KIMBAP
Made Easy

KIMBAP
Made Easy

Recipe Factory

Hollym

Carlsbad, CA and Seoul

KIMBAP Made Easy

Copyright © 2024 by Recipe Factory
All rights reserved.

Publisher	Rhimm Sangbek
Director	Lim Songhee
Editing	Hahm Minji
Design	Lee Hyehee
Translation	Kim Hyunkyung
Proofreading	Richard Harris

First published in 2024
by Hollym International Corp., Carlsbad, CA, USA
Phone 760 814 9880
www.hollym.com   **e-Mail** contact@hollym.com

 Hollym

Published simultaneously in Korea
by Hollym Corp., Publishers, Seoul, Korea
Phone +82 2 734 5087   **Fax** +82 2 730 5149
www.hollym.net   **e-Mail** hollym@hollym.co.kr

ISBN 978-1-56591-526-8
Library of Congress Control Number 2024936179

Printed in Korea

CONTENTS

CHAPTER 1   Basic Kimbap

- Prepare the Laver & Kimbap Roller ··· 15
- Cooking Soft, Fluffy Rice ··· 16
- Seasoning the Cooked Rice ··· 20
- Combining Fillings ··· 22
- Prepare Delicious Fillings ··· 24
- Rolling & Rolling ··· 31

- Regular Kimbap ··· 32
- Premiun King Kimbap ··· 36
- Nude Kimbap ··· 38
- Egg Roll Kimbap ··· 40
- Water Drop Kimbap ··· 42
- Mini Kimbap ··· 44
- Square Kimbap ··· 44

- Neatly Slicing ··· 46
- Pack It Nicely ··· 47

Make It Extra Special
- Enjoying Leftover Ingredients & Kimbap ··· 48

CONTENTS

CHAPTER 2 Non-spicy Kimbap

- Family Kimbap ··· 52
- Chicken Breast & Coleslaw Kimbap ··· 54
- Asparagus Kimbap ··· 56
- Flower Kimbap ··· 58
- Kabocha Squash & Tteokgalbi Kimbap ··· 60
- Smiley Kimbap ··· 62
- Smoked Duck Nude Kimbap ··· 64
- Bassak Bulgogi & Water Parsley Kimbap ··· 66
- Pork Cutlet Kimbap ··· 68
- Omelet Rice Kimbap ··· 70
- Avocado & Crab Meat Kimbap ··· 72
- Teriyaki Shrimp Kimbap ··· 74
- Sprout Salad & Tuna Kimbap ··· 76
- Eel Kimbap ··· 78
- Salmon Kimbap ··· 80
- Cucumber Cream Cheese Nude Kimbap ··· 82
- Pollock Roe Kimbap ··· 84
- Namul Kimbap ··· 86
- Addictive Kimbap ··· 88
- Buckwheat Kimbap ··· 90

Make It Extra Special

- Perfect Side Dishes for a Kimbap Lunch Box ··· 92

CHAPTER 3 Slightly Spicy Kimbap

- Seasoned Fried Chicken Kimbap ··· 94
- Burger Kimbap ··· 96
- Garlic Chives & Bacon Kimbap ··· 98
- Jeyuk Ssam Kimbap ··· 100
- Jangjorim Kimbap ··· 102
- Seasoned Yellow Pickled Radish Kimbap ··· 104
- Spam Egg Roll ··· 106
- Dried Radish Strips Kimbap ··· 108
- Mukeunji Kimbap ··· 110
- Dried Squid Strip Kimbap ··· 112
- Chungmu Kimbap ··· 114
- Tofu Kimchi Kimbap ··· 116

Make It Extra Special
- Using Side Dishes from the Fridge as Kimbap Ingredients ··· 118

CHAPTER 4 Extra Spicy Kimbap

- Spicy Yakgochujang Kimbap ··· 120
- Chili Tuna Kimbap ··· 122
- Hot Squid Kimbap ··· 124
- Spicy Fish Cake Kimbap ··· 126
- Myeolchu Kimbap ··· 128
- Spicy Nuts Kimbap ··· 130
- Ttaengcho Kimbap ··· 132

Make It Extra Special
- Soups to Pair with Spicy Kimbap ··· 134

Three Basic Points for Delicious Kimbap

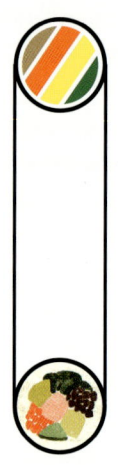

1
The Basis of Kimbap Is Soft, Fluffy Rice!

Rice should be properly cooked to be soft and fluffy so that neither it nor the laver becomes soggy when seasonings and vinegar mixture are mixed in and around it. It is also easier to spread the rice evenly over the laver if it is cooked this way.

2
Mix and Match the Tastes and Textures of the Ingredients!

Choose the main ingredients according to your own personal taste, but try to combine additional salty ingredients with sweeter main ones, or crunchy ones with softer main ingredients, so that the flavors and textures of the ingredients work well together.

3
Remember to Make It Look Nice!

Quality kimbap should look as good as it tastes. When rolling kimbap, place the filling on the top third of the spread-out rice so that the filling is centered in the middle when completed.

Spoon & Cup Measuring Guide

Accurate measurements are essential for delicious kimbap, no matter who's making it.
If you don't have a measuring spoon, a rice spoon will do the trick in a similar way.

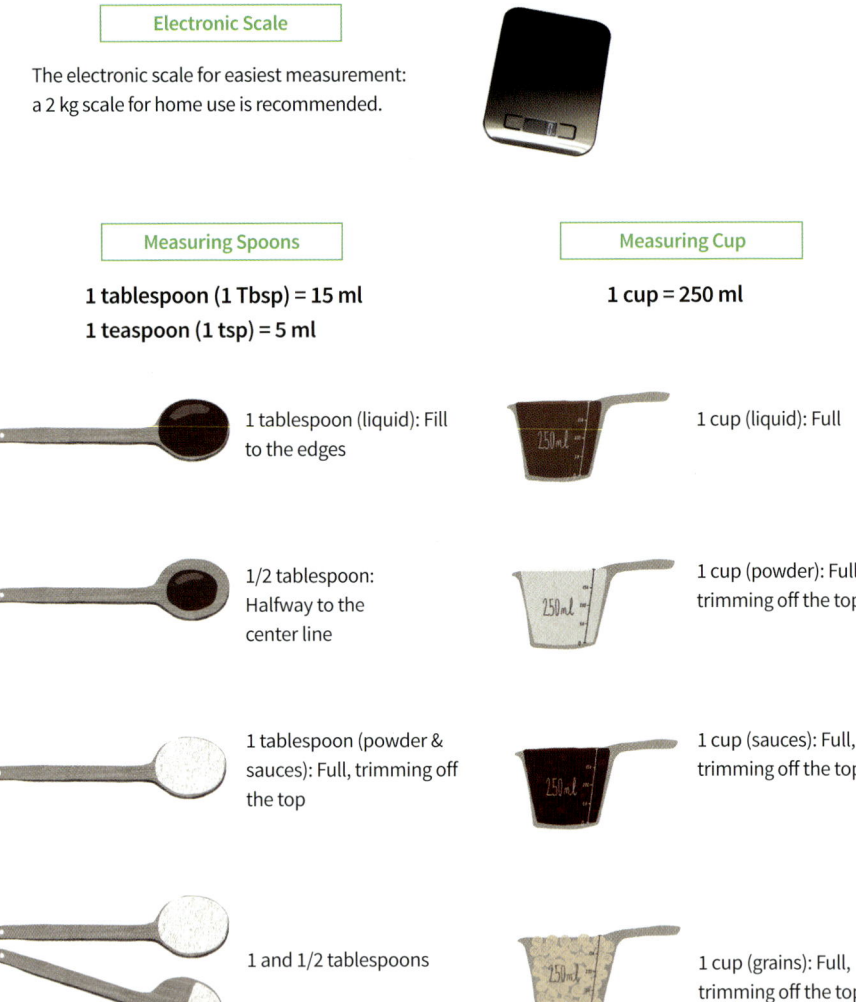

Electronic Scale

The electronic scale for easiest measurement:
a 2 kg scale for home use is recommended.

Measuring Spoons

1 tablespoon (1 Tbsp) = 15 ml
1 teaspoon (1 tsp) = 5 ml

1 tablespoon (liquid): Fill to the edges

1/2 tablespoon: Halfway to the center line

1 tablespoon (powder & sauces): Full, trimming off the top

1 and 1/2 tablespoons

Measuring Cup

1 cup = 250 ml

1 cup (liquid): Full

1 cup (powder): Full, trimming off the top

1 cup (sauces): Full, trimming off the top

1 cup (grains): Full, trimming off the top

Hand-Measurement Guide

For seafood that requires a scale, measure by number or cup, and for vegetables of different sizes, it's helpful to know the number or portions measured by hand.

1 whole pumpkin
(1 kg)

1 piece of radish
(100 g), sliced

1 avocado
(200 g)

1 asparagus spear
(13 g)

1 carrot
(200 g)

1 cucumber
(200 g)

1 fistful water parsley
(70 g)

1 fistful garlic chives
(50 g)

1 fistful spinach
(50 g)

1 slice chicken tenderloin
(25 g)

1 cup napa cabbage kimchi
(190 g)

1 cup walnuts
(140 g)

Ingredient Preparation Guide

Kimbap is flavored with the harmony of various ingredients. As a general rule, the more carefully the ingredients are prepared, the better the kimbap will taste. Here's how to prepare some of the more uncommon ingredients for kimbap.

Avocado

Using a large, sharp knife, cut the avocado lengthwise around the seed. Open the two halves to expose the pit. Use a spoon to scoop out the pit, or tap the edge of the knife into the pit and then twist the pit out of the avocado and discard the pit. You can then either scoop out the avocado flesh with a spoon or slice it into segments.

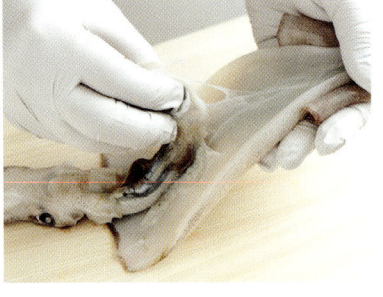

Squid

Body Cut in half with scissors and pull off the tentacles (with the intestines attached) by hand, removing the transparent bone inside.

Tentacles Cut out the intestines and put them under running water to remove the suckers.

Asparagus

Remove the base (1 cm) and peel with a peeler.

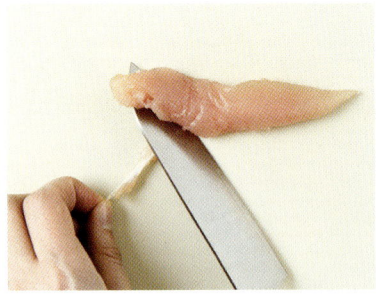

Chicken Tenderloin

Remove the white sinew with a knife.

CHAPTER 1

Basic Kimbap

A Complete Beginner's Guide to Conquering Basic Kimbap

Making Kimbap Step by Step

We'll walk you through the process of making kimbap step by step
and in easy-to-follow detail. At the end of each step,
you'll find useful tips for your own personalized kimbap.

Prepare the Laver & Kimbap Roller

It's not just about flavor. It's also about making sure your kimbap stays nice and firm. Take note before you tackle the rolling stage.

Laver for Kimbap

Characteristics
This kind of laver is thicker, denser, and tougher than regular laver, so it doesn't tear easily when rolling kimbap. Roasted laver is highly recommended, as you can enjoy its savory flavor and crispy texture.

Use
The laver is shiny on the front and dull on the back, with a relatively rough surface. Place the laver with the rough side facing up and spread the rice on top to create a smooth texture when your kimbap is completed.

Storage
Store leftover laver for kimbap in a seal top bag in the freezer, sealed tightly (up to 3 months). However, it's best to use it as soon as possible because it can turn red from moisture if stored for a long period of time.

When Laver Becomes Soggy
You can bring back the crispness of laver by roasting each sheet on a dry pan for 30 seconds on each side. In a microwave (700W), put it in for 30 seconds, then flip it over and microwave for another 30 seconds.

Kimbap Roller

Bamboo Kimbap Roller

Features
If you choose a roller with a tightly spaced bamboo weave, you can make your kimbap a little firmer.

Cleaning & Storing
Soak the roller in water for 5 minutes, then wash it thoroughly without dishwashing liquid and dry it completely in the shade to prevent bacteria from growing. Roll it up and store it.

Silicon Kimbap Roller

Features
Although easy to clean and rice doesn't stick to it, it's a little less powerful than a bamboo kimbap roller when it comes to rolling kimbap firmly.

Cleaning & Storing
Wash with dishwashing liquid, dry, and roll up to store.

Cooking Soft, Fluffy Rice

Rice should be properly cooked to be soft and fluffy so that neither it nor the laver becomes soggy when seasonings and vinegar mixture are mixed in and around it. This makes for a good kimbap texture. It's also easier to spread this kind of rice evenly over the laver, so the shape of finished kimbap looks beautiful.

When Cooking Only Non-glutinous Rice

For the most flavorful rice, you need to first soak the rice well.
Check the soaking time depending on the condition of the rice.

1

Place rice in a bowl, add water, and rinse to lightly clean it. Add enough water to cover and soak for 30 minutes (1 hour for older rice).

▶ If you soak the rice too long, it may make the grains break and the cooked rice will be too soft.

▶ Remember the ratio of soaked rice: water = 1:1. Reduce the amount of water by 10% when using fresh rice, which contains a lot of moisture, or increase the amount of water by 10% when using older rice.

2

Drain the rice in a sieve and add an equal amount of water to the rice. If using an electric rice cooker, select the "White Rice" or "Multigrain Rice" mode.

If using a pot, add the rice and water, put the lid on, bring to a boil over high heat, then reduce heat to medium and simmer for 5 minutes. Simmer for another 10 minutes over very low heat, then turn off the heat and let sit for 2 minutes before mixing well.

▶ After cooking, let the hot steam cool to remove the moisture so the cooked rice becomes fluffier.

How Much Rice Does It Take to Make a Kimbap Roll?

Here's a handy formula to remember.

 = =  = =

| 1 cup (250 g) rice | 1½ bowls (300 g) cooked rice | regular kimbap (150 g) × 2 rolls | premium king kimbap (100 g) × 3 rolls | mini kimbap (25 g) × 12 rolls |

When Cooking Multigrain Rice

If you change the type of cooked rice, you can enjoy different tastes to your kimbap. The recipes in this book are based on non-glutinous rice, but you can change the type of cooked rice according to your taste.

	Non-glutinous Rice + Black Rice	Non-glutinous Rice + Brown Rice	Non-glutinous Rice + Glutinous Rice
Features	If fillings are mostly light-colored, you can add an interesting visual feature to kimbap with black rice.	Mixing in brown rice that is healthy and pleasant to chew makes kimbap that is soft and fluffy in texture.	This is characterized by a sticky and chewy texture and is delicious even when cooled. It goes well with fillings such as *namul* (seasoned herbal dishes), *mukeunji*, and *tteokgalbi*.
Ratio	**Non-glutinous rice: Black rice = 2:1**	**Non-glutinous rice: Brown rice = 9:1** Starting with a ratio of 9:1, which many people prefer, you can increase the amount of brown rice to your liking.	**Non-glutinous rice: Glutinous rice = 8:2**
Recipe	Mix the black rice with the non-glutinous rice and cook the rice in the same way as you would for regular cooked rice (see page 17).	For brown rice, soak it for 5–6 hours before cooking. You can reduce the soaking time by using glutinous brown rice.	Because glutinous rice contains a lot of water, reduce the amount of water to 1:0.8, and cook the rice the same way you would for regular cooked rice (see page 17).

Want Brighter, More Flavorful Rice?

When cooking rice, add 1 piece of kelp (5×5 cm) to the rice and water for a brighter, more flavorful rice.

When making kimbap, the cooked rice is mushy. Is there any way to fix this?

1. Place the cooked rice in a heatproof container and microwave (700W) for 30 seconds, uncovered, to loosen the moisture. Spread the rice out and let cool slightly before seasoning.

2. You can also use store-bought instant rice by heating it up in a microwave and mixing it into the mushy rice.

3. Season the cooked rice with salt, sesame seeds, and sesame oil. When seasoning the rice with a vinegar mixture, it can make the rice wet.

4. After adding the seasoning, mix the rice lightly, as overmixing can cause the grains to break up. Using a wooden spatula will help to release the moisture and make the rice fluffier.

Seasoning the Cooked Rice

There are two common rice seasonings for kimbap—basic seasoning and a vinegar mixture—but there are many other flavors you can use to suit your choice of fillings and taste preferences.

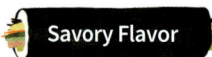

Basic Seasonings (salt, sesame seeds, sesame oil/perilla oil)
These usually go well with Korean-style kimbap, herbs, and side dishes.

Mayonnaise
Recommended not only for instant kimbap but also for neutralizing the taste of salty or spicy ingredients.

Brewed Soy Sauce & Butter
Perfect for kimbap made with *jangjorim* (braised beef in soy sauce) and kimbap for kids.

Vinegar Mixture Seasoning (vinegar, sugar, salt)
Common with kimbap for picnics/takeout or in summer; fusion kimbap with salmon, crab meat, or any other fish.

Teriyaki
Suitable for kimbap made with eel, pork cutlet, or any other similar ingredient.

Ketchup, Curry Powder, Dried Herbs, and Furikake
Perfect for kids' kimbap and recommended for kimbap with an out-of-the-ordinary flavor!

Sesame Oil vs Perilla Oil: Similar but Different!

Sesame oil, which comes from pressing sesame seeds, is mostly made up of unsaturated fatty acids. It has a longer shelf life than perilla oil and can be stored at room temperature. Perilla oil, which comes from pressing perilla seeds, is rich in omega-3 fatty acids, but it's more susceptible to oxidation, so store it in a dark bottle and refrigerate. It goes rancid quickly, so it's best to use it on kimbap that will be eaten immediately.

The Two Most Common Seasonings

Basic Seasoning

Ingredients

- 2 tsp whole sesame seeds (or black sesame seeds)
- ½ tsp salt
- 2 tsp sesame oil (or perilla oil)

Seasoning

1. In a large bowl, place the warm, fully cooked rice (1½ bowls, 300 g) and add the sesame seeds, salt, and sesame oil.
2. Using a wooden spatula, quickly mix the rice horizontally and vertically to break up any lumps. For a fluffy texture, don't press the rice.
   ▶ If you use a wooden spatula, the wood will absorb the moisture from the rice and help make it fluffy.

Notes

- Season the cooked rice while it's still warm so that the cooked rice is evenly seasoned.
- Kimbap becomes less salty as it sits, so if you're making it for a lunch box, you may want to season it with a touch of salt.
- If your kimbap fillings are salty, reduce the amount of salt in the seasoning for the cooked rice.

Vinegar Mixture Seasoning

Ingredients

- 1 Tbsp vinegar
- 2 tsp sugar (to taste)
- ⅓ tsp salt

Seasoning

1. In a large bowl, whisk together the vinegar, sugar, and salt to dissolve the sugar and salt.
2. Add the warm, fully cooked rice (1½ bowls, 300 g) to the bowl in ①.
3. Using a wooden spatula, quickly mix the rice horizontally and vertically to avoid any lumps.

Notes

- The vinegar mixture should be made in advance so that the salt and sugar dissolve and the cooked rice is evenly seasoned.
- In summer, you can add green plum syrup to the vinegar mixture for better preservation. When this is done, reduce the amount of vinegar and sugar slightly.

Combining Fillings

First, choose the main ingredients. If the main ingredients are sweet, then combine salty additional ingredients. If the main ingredients tend to be soft, combine crunchy additional ingredients with them so that the flavors and textures of all the fillings go well together.

Flavor Ingredients

Salty
Bacon, braised burdock root, dried squid strips, fish cake, ham, salted pollock roe, small anchovies, smoked duck, *tteokgalbi*, yellow pickled radish

Sweet
Braised burdock root, onion, sliced pickled radish, yellow pickled radish

Sour
Kimchi, pickled green pepper, *rakkyo zuke* (Japanese scallion pickles), sliced pickled radish, yellow pickled radish, other types of pickles

Spicy/Tangy
Cheongyang chili peppers, dried radish strips, garlic chives, jalapenos, kimchi, onion, pickled green pepper, stir-fried *gochujang*

Savory
Cream cheese, nuts, potatoes, sliced cheese

Textural Ingredients

Crunchy
Asparagus, bell pepper, braised burdock, cabbage, carrot, cucumber, dried radish strips, *mukeunji* (well-aged kimchi), onion, paprika, yellow pickled radish

Soft
Avocado, cheese, crab meat, egg, fish cake, ham, shrimp, tofu

Chewy
Agaric mushrooms, dried squid strips, squid

Crispy
Deep-fried shrimp, pork cutlet

Fragrant Ingredients

Chwinamul (aster scaber), leek, perilla leaf, water parsley

Ingredients that neutralize the spiciness

Cabbage, cheese, egg, mayonnaise, tofu, tuna

Alternatives to yellow pickled radish

A variety of pickles (carrot, onion, cucumber, green pepper), jalapenos, *mukeunji*, *rakkyo zuke* (Japanese scallion pickles), sliced pickled radish

Seasonings and watery ingredients

After squeezing out the seasonings or water from the ingredients, wrap them in leaves or lettuce first, then roll them in laver for a cleaner look.

Ingredients for more careful use in summer

Ingredients such as meat, *namul*, spinach, and tofu tend to spoil quickly in the heat of the day, so use them only in kimbap that will be eaten immediately. In the summer, cucumber is recommended instead of spinach.

Prepare Delicious Fillings

Properly preparing and cooking all the fillings is essential for making them evenly seasoned. Take a look at these tips for preparing the most common ingredients in kimbap and then prepare your own!

Spinach

For 4 regular kimbap rolls
(4 fistfuls spinach, 200 g)

1. Remove the messy leaves from the spinach, cut off the roots with a knife, and tear the spinach leaves apart.
2. Blanch the spinach stem side down first in boiling water (8 cups water + 2 tsp salt) for 30 seconds. Rinse under cold water and squeeze out the water.
3. Toss with salt (½ tsp) and sesame oil (1 tsp).
   - ▶ For longer, tougher fillings like spinach, dried squid strips, and garlic chives, cut them into 2 or 3 pieces beforehand for easier slicing of kimbap.

Carrot

For 4 regular kimbap rolls
(½ carrot, 100 g)

1. Peel the carrot with a peeler and shred it.
2. Add cooking oil (1 tsp) to a hot pan, add carrot, salt (a little), and stir-fry for 2 minutes over medium heat.
   - ▶ If you stir-fry the other ingredients after stir-frying the carrot, the color may change, so stir-fry the carrot last.

> The seeds have a lot of water in them, so it's best to remove them!

Burdock Root

For 4 regular kimbap rolls
(2 cm diameter, 10 cm length, 25 g)

1. Peel the burdock root with a peeler and cut it into long, 0.5 cm thick slices.
2. Soak in vinegar water (2 cups water + 1 Tbsp vinegar) for 10 minutes to remove acerbity and prevent browning.
3. Blanch the burdock root in boiling water (3 cups water + 1 tsp salt) for 2 minutes.
4. In a saucepan, combine the cooking wine (½ Tbsp), sugar (1 tsp), brewed soy sauce (2 tsp), and ⅖ cup (100 ml) of water, bring to a boil, add the burdock root, and cook over medium-low heat for 1 minute, pouring the mixed seasoning over it.
   ▶ To reduce the salty flavor of store-bought braised burdock root, you can place it in a sieve and rinse it under running water to drain before using.

Cucumber

For 4 regular kimbap rolls
(½ cucumber, 100 g)

Rub the outside of the cucumber with salt (1 Tbsp), rinse under running water, and remove the spikes on the surface with a knife. Cut off the bitter ends.

1. **For long pieces** Cut lengthwise into quarters and remove the seeds.
2. **For slices** Cut the trimmed cucumber into two halves and slice on three sides, as shown in the photo below. Remove seeds and finely shred, toss with salt (½ tsp), and let sit for 10 minutes. Drain in a sieve and rinse under cold water, then wrap in paper towels to remove any leftover water.

| Yellow Pickled Radish | Ground Beef |

1. Drain in a sieve and rinse under running water.
2. Drain in a sieve.
   ▶ Store-bought yellow pickled radish often contains additives to improve texture and color, but rinsing it in water removes as much of the water-soluble additives as possible.

For 4 regular kimbap rolls (200 g beef)

1. Wrap the beef in a paper towel to drain the blood.
2. In a bowl, combine the brewed soy sauce (1 Tbsp), sugar (½ Tbsp), minced garlic (1 tsp), sesame oil (1 tsp), and black pepper (a pinch), then add the beef and toss to coat.
3. Add cooking oil (1 tsp) to a hot pan, add ② and stir-fry until seasoning disappears and the beef becomes soft and fluffy.
4. Place on a paper towel or sieve to remove as much moisture as possible.

| Fish Cake, Ham, Smoked Duck | Crab Meat |

1. Blanch these ingredients in boiling water for 1 minute, or drain in a sieve with 1 cup (250 ml) of hot water.
   ▶ If you blanch or pour in hot water to drain the oil, you will ensure more mild-tasting food.

1. For short crab meat pieces, tear it into thin strips by hand.
2. For long crab meat pieces, cut it in half lengthwise. Add cooking oil (1 tsp) to a hot pan and stir-fry for 1 minute over medium heat, then let cool slightly.

Tips to Remember When Preparing Your Fillings!

Drain as much water as possible to keep the laver from becoming soggy and the kimbap from spoiling easily. Add hot ingredients only after letting them cool slightly to prevent the laver from shrinking.

Choose Your Favorite Style of Egg

Eggs are one of the most important ingredients in kimbap!
You can add thick or thin slices of fried egg according to your taste.

> **Chunky Egg Strip**

For 3 to 4 regular kimbap rolls
- 3 eggs
- 1 tsp cooking wine
- ⅓ tsp salt
- 1 tsp cooking oil

1. Combine all the ingredients in a bowl and whisk. Add cooking oil to a hot pan and spread evenly with a paper towel.
   ▶ Wipe the pan with a paper towel and cook over low heat so that the eggs don't bubble and are smooth.

2. Pour in ½ of the egg wash and cook over low heat until 80% done (until the egg wash on the top is no longer running) and fold into 5–6 cm wide strips.
   ▶ If it's over 80% cooked, the finished egg strip will fall apart when you cut with a knife and it won't have a nice shape.

3. Continue to pour in the egg wash and fold to thicken.
   ▶ You can also add 1 more egg to make it thicker.

4. While hot, place on a kimbap roller and press firmly to shape. Let it cool slightly and cut into 3 or 4 pieces.

It has a nice, fluffy texture~

Shredded Egg

For 2 to 3 regular kimbap rolls

- 2 eggs
- a pinch of salt
- 1 tsp cooking oil

1. Whisk the eggs and salt in a bowl.
2. Add cooking oil to a hot pan and spread evenly with a paper towel.
3. Pour in the egg wash and cook over low heat for 1 minute, then flip with a large spatula or long wooden chopsticks, and cook for 30 seconds.
4. Let it all cool slightly, then cut into 2 pieces and finely shred them.
   - ▶ You can also make wide egg strips by slicing them according to your desired size (see pages 58, 70, and 96).

It blends better with the other ingredients~

It's Convenient to Use a Square Pan for Frying Eggs!

Use a square pan to make a clean, easy, and waste-free egg strip, and then shred.

6

Rolling & Rolling

Even if you use the same ingredients,
changing the way you roll kimbap can make it feel like a different kind of kimbap!
This section shows you how to make a variety of kimbap—
from regular kimbap to nude kimbap to mini kimbap for kids.

Regular Kimbap

1 roll = 150 g cooked rice
Basic kimbap with half fillings and half rice

1. Place the laver rough side up on the kimbap roller and add the cooked rice (150 g). Lightly moisten your fingers with water (or cooking oil) and spread the rice grains by pushing them together. Spread the rice only ¾ of the way across the laver.
   - ▶ Allow the cooked rice to cool slightly before rolling to prevent the laver from being moistened and grains from sticking to your hands.
   - ▶ Spreading the rice grains evenly and flatly will ensure that the fillings are not disordered and that the kimbap looks nice.
   - ▶ Use only a little water on your fingers, as too much water will make the rice mushy.

2. Place the fillings on the cooked rice ⅓ of the way up.
   - ▶ Make sure that the similarly colored ingredients do not overlap so that the finished kimbap has a nice cross-section.

3   Hold the kimbap roller with your thumbs and index fingers, and the fillings with the rest of your fingers, then roll the kimbap roller while pressing firmly.
   ▶ If the fillings come out on the side, gently push them back in and roll the kimbap.

4   When the ends of the cooked rice meet, gently pull the kimbap roller upward to further adhere the fillings to the rice.

5 Place small rice grain clusters 2–3 cm apart on the end of the laver and crush them with your hands or apply a little water.

6 Roll with the kimbap roller, as shown in the photo, pressing firmly to shape.

There's a Correct Order in which to Add the Ingredients, too!

If you add shredded ingredients (e.g., carrot, cucumber, egg) last, they become easy to fall apart during the rolling process. As a general rule, the order of ingredients is "spread (salted pollock roe, pumpkin salad, tuna) → shredded ingredients → chunky ingredients (e.g., pork cutlet, smoked duck, *tteokgalbi*)," but you can change the order depending on the overall color or shape. Also, if the ingredients are too big, it's hard to roll the kimbap into a circular form, so cut the pork cutlet or *tteokgalbi* into 2–3 cm thick pieces.

7. Pick up the kimbap wrapped in the roller and press it firmly with two hands.
   - ▶ Be careful. If you apply too much pressure, the texture of the kimbap roller will be imprinted on the kimbap.
   - ▶ Be careful with soft ingredients such as sweet pumpkin salad and tuna because they may spill out.

8. Brush evenly with sesame oil (1 tsp), put the seam side of the laver facing down, and let sit for 5 minutes.
   - ▶ You need to let it sit for a minute or so before slicing to prevent the ends of the laver from unraveling.

I'm basic. :)

Premium King Kimbap

1 roll = 100 g cooked rice
A gourmet kind of kimbap with more fillings than rice

1 Cut 1 laver sheet in half.

2 Place small rice grain clusters on the bottom 1 cm of the cut laver and crush it, then attach another piece of laver (1 sheet).

Use your hands to push in both ends so that the fillings don't slide out.

3. Place the laver rough side up on the kimbap roller and add cooked rice (100 g). Lightly moisten your fingers with water (or cooking oil) and spread the rice by pushing it all together. Spread the rice only ¾ of the way across the laver.

4. Add some more fillings than usual and roll it in the same way as regular kimbap (see page 32).

Plenty of fillings!

Nude Kimbap

1 roll = 150 g cooked rice
Unconventional kimbap with rice on the outside

1. Wrap the front and back of the kimbap roller tightly with plastic wrap.
   - ▶ If you wrap the entire kimbap roller in plastic wrap before rolling the kimbap, the rice grains will not stick to the roller.

2. Place laver on the kimbap roller and add rice (150 g). Lightly moisten your fingers with water (or cooking oil) and spread the rice grains by pushing them together. Spread the rice so that it protrudes 0.5–1 cm beyond the end of the laver.
   - ▶ The rice grains should be evenly distributed from top to bottom so that the finished kimbap looks neat and pretty.

3. Flip the laver over so that the rice is down, and place the fillings on top of the laver ⅓ of the way up.

4. Use a wrapped kimbap roller to roll up.
   ▶ Nude kimbap needs to be rolled tighter than regular kimbap so the fillings don't fall out when you slice it.

Think differently~

Egg Roll Kimbap

1 roll = 150 g cooked rice
Completed kimbap wrapped in a soft egg crepe

1. In a small bowl, beat the eggs (3 eggs, for 2 rolls of kimbap) well.
   ▶ You can also use a sieve to remove the chalazae to get an even softer texture.

2. Place the cooking oil (1 tsp) in a pan heated over low heat and spread the oil evenly over the pan, slightly wiping it off with a paper towel. Pour in the egg wash and tilt the pan to spread it across the pan.

3 When half-cooked to an opaque color over low heat, place the kimbap on the edge of the egg and roll up with a spatula and chopsticks.
- ▶ If the egg is fully cooked, it's not rolled, so add the kimbap when it is halfway done.
- ▶ You can also sprinkle the egg with shredded pizza cheese before rolling the kimbap (see page 107).

4 Use a kimbap roller to firmly shape the kimbap, then let cool slightly before slicing.

I'm dressed in a soft egg~

Water Drop Kimbap

1 roll = 150 g cooked rice
A type of kimbap that looks like a water drop alone and a pretty flower when put together

1. Roll out the cooked rice and add the fillings as you would for regular kimbap (see page 32). Fold the kimbap roller so that the ends of the rice meet and form a water drop shape, as shown in the photo.

2. Place small rice grain clusters 2–3 cm apart on the end of the laver and crush them with your hands or apply a little water.

3. Lower the kimbap roller and flip the kimbap by hand.

4. Reshape the kimbap with the kimbap roller.

I'll be a flower~

Mini Kimbap

1 roll = 25 g cooked rice
A small type of kimbap that fits easily
into a child's mouth

1. Cut the laver into quarters and place 2 Tbsp of the cooked rice ¾ of the way across the laver. Place the fillings on ⅓ of the rice.
   ▶ To make the kimbap child-friendly, shred or cut the fillings into half portions and roll with only 2–3 ingredients.
2. Roll the kimbap, then slice it to make the kimbap easier to eat.

Bite-sized~

Square Kimbap

1 roll = 150 g cooked rice
A kind of square kimbap that fits nicely
in a lunch box

1. Complete one roll of kimbap (see page 32).
2. Place the kimbap roller on top of the kimbap, as shown in the photo, to make it square-shaped.

I'm special!

One side of the kimbap has burst.

1

Cut a piece of laver roughly the size of the tear.
Lightly moisten the laver on all sides with a cooking brush or your fingers.

2

Place the laver over the burst area and wrap it with the kimbap roller, tightly attaching it.
Leave the attached laver side down for 5 minutes before slicing.
▶ You can also make egg roll kimbap wrapped in an egg crepe (see page 40).

Neatly Slicing

Once you've rolled the kimbap nice and tight, it's time to neatly slice it.
The trick is to go back and forth, like in a sawing motion,
while wiping your knife every few cuts.

After wiping the blade clean, soak a paper towel in sesame oil or vinegar water (2 cups water + 1 tsp vinegar) and wipe the knife with it.

Slice the kimbap into 1.5 cm wide pieces by moving the knife back and forth as if sawing. Coat the blade with sesame oil or vinegar water intermittently while slicing.
▶ Wiping the blade while slicing makes it neater.

Pack It Nicely

You've been up since the crack of dawn preparing kimbap. It's frustrating to open the lid of your lunch box with excitement only to find that the slices of kimbap are sticking together and making a mess. To finish the job, learn how to pack your rice perfectly.

After placing the kimbap in a lunch box container, stagger the top rows so they don't overlap. Fill in the empty spaces with food such as other slices of kimbap, cherry tomatoes, hard-boiled quail eggs, or mini hot dogs/sausages to keep the kimbap from wobbling (see page 92).

Pack your kimbap in a special container so it doesn't lose its shape.
► You can also sprinkle with sesame seeds to garnish.

Add Sauces!

You can add sauces to your kimbap to give it a different flavor. You can also decorate it. Try ketchup (page 62), mayonnaise (page 78), mustard (page 88), and chili sauce, or be adventurous and try something else!

Make It Extra Special

Enjoying Leftover Ingredients & Kimbap

Recommended when you have a lot of leftover ingredients or kimbap.

Morning Sandwiches with Kimbap Fillings

⏱ 20–30 minutes / 4 pieces

- 4 morning rolls
  (or 4 slices plain bread)
- leftover kimbap ingredients
  (crab meat, cucumber, ham for
  kimbap, carrot, etc., 120 g)
- 1 lettuce leaf (palm size, 15 g)
- 2 cheese slices (optional)
- 1 tsp cooking oil

Sauce
- 1½ Tbsp mayonnaise
- 1 Tbsp mustard
- ½ Tbsp oligofructose
- 1 tsp lemon juice (or vinegar)
- a pinch of salt

❶ Cut the kimbap ingredients into 0.5 cm pieces on all sides.
  ▶ You can also shred the ingredients.

❷ Add cooking oil to a hot pan, then add crab meat and ham for the kimbap and stir-fry over medium heat for 2 minutes, then let cool slightly.

❸ Wrap lettuce in paper towels to remove any leftover water, then tear it into slices with your hands.
  ▶ Remove as much water as possible to prevent soggy bread.

❹ Insert a long knife into the center of each morning roll, ⅔ of the way through. Cut the sliced cheese diagonally into 2 pieces and peel off the cover.

❺ In a bowl, mix ① and ② and the sauce ingredients.

❻ Top each morning roll with sliced cheese, ¼ of the lettuce, and ⑤.

Transforming Leftover Kimbap into Stir-Fried Rice

⏱ **20–30 minutes / 2 servings**
- 2 kimbap rolls
- 120 g ripe napa cabbage kimchi
- 2 eggs
- 1 tsp cooking oil
- 1 Tbsp chili oil (or cooking oil)
- 2 tsp oyster sauce
  (add or subtract as desired, or make optional)
- 2 tsp sesame oil

❶ Cut the kimbap into bite-sized pieces. Mince the kimchi into 1 cm pieces on all sides.

❷ Add cooking oil to a hot pan, then add the eggs and cook for 2 minutes over medium-low heat so it's half-cooked, and set aside.

❸ Wipe the pan clean with a paper towel, reheat, add the chili oil and kimchi, and stir-fry over medium-low heat for 2 minutes. Then add the kimbap and stir-fry for 2 minutes, breaking it up with a spatula.

❹ Add the oyster sauce and stir-fry for 1 minute, then turn off the heat and mix in the sesame oil.

❺ Top with a fried egg.

CHAPTER 2

Non-spicy Kimbap

A Variety of Casual Favorites for All Ages

Family Kimbap

Let's make faces of a happy family using kimbap! We made faces out of egg rolls and decorated them with laver and carrot. You and your child can come up with different ideas to represent your family's faces!

30–40 minutes / 2 rolls (1 roll = 426 kcal)
- 1 bowl (200 g) warm cooked rice
- 2 laver sheets + 1 extra laver sheet (for the egg roll)
- 10 g carrot
- 3 tsp cooking oil

Egg Roll
- 6 eggs
- 2 tsp sugar
- 1/3 tsp salt
- 2 tsp cooking wine

Cooked Rice Seasoning
- 1 Tbsp vinegar
- 2 tsp sugar
- 1/3 tsp salt

Garnishes
- Laver or black sesame seeds
- a dash of ketchup

Preparing the Ingredients

1. **Laver (for the egg roll)** Cut 1 sheet in half.
   Eggs In a bowl, mix the egg roll ingredients.
   Carrot Finely shred it. Add cooking oil (1 tsp) to a hot pan and stir-fry for 2 minutes over medium heat (see page 24).

2. Add cooking oil (1 tsp) to a hot pan, spread with a paper towel, and pour in half of the egg wash. Tilt the pan to evenly distribute the egg wash and cook over low heat for 1 minute. Flip over and roll tightly with chopsticks and a spatula to a 3 cm diameter, then let it cool slightly.

3. Make a slit in the egg roll, then open the slit slightly and insert half of the shredded carrot in the center. Repeat for 1 more egg roll.

4. Place the egg roll on the laver from ① and roll up.
   ▶ If you roll the egg roll once in the laver, the faces will look clearer when you finish the kimbap.

Seasoning the Cooked Rice

In a large bowl, stir the rice seasoning ingredients until the sugar and salt dissolve, then add the cooked rice, mix, and let cool slightly.

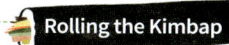 **Rolling the Kimbap**

Spread the cooked rice (½ portion) ¾ of the way across the laver.

↓

Top with 1 egg roll and roll up.

↓

Make 1 more roll and cut into bite-sized pieces.

↓

Garnishing

Create facial expressions with laver or black sesame seeds, ketchup, etc.
▶ You can also use tweezers, toothpicks, or a laver puncher for more delicate decorations.

▶ **Laver puncher**
Simply put the laver between the punchers and press down to make the shapes shown in the picture. Laver punchers are available at major supermarkets and online stores.

Add Sliced Cheese

You can also finely chop 1 slice of cheese and mix it in with the egg roll ingredients, then follow the same steps the rest of the way.

Chicken Breast & Coleslaw Kimbap

This crunchy, chewy kimbap is made with red cabbage and a generous helping of sweet and sour coleslaw. The sweet and salty grilled chicken breast with soy sauce and refreshing tomato make this especially great in summer.

⏱ 40–50 minutes / 2 rolls (1 roll = 428 kcal)
- 1½ bowls (300 g) warm cooked rice
- 2 laver sheets
- 1 chicken breast (or 4 chicken tenderloins, 100 g)
- 4 red cabbage leaves (palm size, or cabbage, 120 g)
- ⅔ tomato
- ⅓ carrot
- 4 perilla leaves
- 1 Tbsp cooking oil
- 1 Tbsp mayonnaise
- ½ tsp mustard (add or subtract as desired)

Coleslaw Seasoning
- 1 Tbsp sugar
- 1½ Tbsp vinegar
- ½ tsp salt

Base Seasoning for Chicken Breast
- ½ tsp minced garlic
- 1 tsp brewed soy sauce
- 1 tsp sugar
- 1 tsp cooking wine
- a pinch of ground black pepper

Cooked Rice Seasoning
- 1 Tbsp vinegar
- 2 tsp salt
- ⅓ tsp salt

Preparing the Ingredients

1. **Red cabbage** Finely mince, toss with coleslaw seasoning, and let sit for 15 minutes, then squeeze out water.

2. **Chicken breast** Halve and slice into 1 cm thick slices. Toss with the base seasoning and let sit for 10 minutes.

3. **Carrots** Shred finely.
   Perilla leaves Remove stems.
   Tomato Remove seeds and cut into 0.5 cm thick slices.

4. Add cooking oil to a hot pan, and cook the chicken breast over medium-low heat until golden brown, 4 to 5 minutes.

5. In a bowl, combine the red cabbage from ①, mayonnaise, and mustard.

Seasoning the Cooked Rice

In a large bowl, stir the rice seasoning ingredients until the sugar and salt dissolve, then add the cooked rice, mix, and let cool slightly.

Using the Coleslaw

Refreshing coleslaw can be served as a salad with kimbap or as a sandwich filling.

Rolling the Kimbap

Spread the cooked rice (½ portion) ¾ of the way across the laver.

↓

Spread 2 perilla leaves and top with coleslaw (½ portion).

↓

Top with chicken breast (½ portion) and shredded carrot (½ portion).

↓

Top with tomato (½ portion) and roll up.

↓

Make 1 more roll and cut into bite-sized pieces.

Asparagus Kimbap

This is a specialty type of kimbap made with cooked rice seasoned with curry powder. It's characterized by its distinctive texture with plenty of crispy asparagus. It's added with grilled bacon, which goes well with asparaguses, and *ssammu*, which adds a sweet and sour flavor.

40–50 minutes / 2 rolls (1 roll = 435 kcal)

- 1½ bowls (300 g) warm cooked rice
- 2 laver sheets
- 10 asparagus spears
- ⅓ carrot
- 4 bacon strips
- 8 slices store-bought *ssammu*
- 1 tsp butter
- a pinch of salt + ⅓ tsp salt
- 1 tsp cooking oil

Cooked Rice Seasoning

- 4 tsp curry powder
- 3 tsp sesame seeds
- 1 tsp sugar
- 2 tsp olive oil

Preparing the Ingredients

1. **Asparagus** Remove the base and peel with a peeler (see page 12).
   Carrot Shred finely.
   Ssammu Squeeze out water.

2. Add butter to a hot pan, add asparaguses and salt (⅓ tsp) and stir-fry over medium heat for 2 minutes, then set aside.
   ▶ You can also blanch them in hot water for 1 minute instead of pan-frying them.

3. Add cooking oil to a pan, add carrot, salt (a pinch), and stir-fry over medium-low heat for 2 minutes, then set aside.

4. Wipe the pan clean with a paper towel, reheat, and add the bacon while cooking over medium heat for 1 minute, each side, then place on paper towels to remove the fat.

Seasoning the Cooked Rice

In a large bowl, mix the cooked rice and the rice seasoning ingredients, then let cool slightly.

Choosing Asparagus

Look for tender, thick stalks with no tough cuts, deep green, fresh leaves, and no bearded roots showing through the stalks.

Rolling the Kimbap

Spread the cooked rice (½ portion) ¾ of the way across the laver.

↓

Spread 4 *ssammu* slices and top with 2 bacon strips.

↓

Top with shredded carrot (½ portion).

↓

Top with 5 asparagus spears and roll up.

↓

Make 1 more roll and cut into bite-sized pieces.

Flower Kimbap

This type of kimbap looks like a pretty flower on a plate. The crispy baked bacon is rolled in an egg crepe to form the flower, and the green spinach is rolled in with it to serve as the petals. To make kimbap with any particular shape, you can make it much more easily by cutting the laver into 2 pieces and rolling the kimbap into short strips.

⏱ **50–60 minutes / 4 short rolls (1 roll = 239 kcal)**

- 1 bowl (200 g) warm cooked rice
- 4 laver sheets (For egg bacon roll, spinach roll)
- 2 fistfuls spinach (100 g)
- 4 eggs
- 4 strips bacon
- ½ tsp salt + a pinch of salt
- 2 tsp sesame oil
- 2 tsp cooking oil

Cooked Rice Seasoning
- 1 Tbsp sugar
- 1 Tbsp vinegar
- ½ tsp salt

Preparing the Ingredients

1. **Spinach** Blanch in boiling water (3 cups water + 1 tsp salt) for 30 seconds, then rinse in cold water and squeeze out water. In a bowl, toss the spinach with salt (½ tsp) and sesame oil.

2. **Bacon** Finely mince.
   Eggs In a bowl, whisk together the eggs and a pinch of salt.

3. **2 Laver sheets**
   Cut into 2 pieces lengthwise.

4. **2 Laver sheets**
   Cut into 2 pieces lengthwise and then into thirds.

5. Add cooking oil (1 tsp) to a hot pan, spread evenly with a paper towel, pour in the egg wash and cook over low heat for 1 minute, then flip and cook for 30 seconds. Make one more egg crepe in the same way and cut into 2 pieces to get 4 rectangular egg strips in total.

6. Reheat the pan, add the minced bacon and cook over medium heat until crisp, 2 minutes. Place the bacon on a paper towel to remove oil.

7. Spread the bacon (¼ portion each) evenly on each of the 4 egg strips from ⑤, roll them up tightly, and wrap each with a laver sheet from ④.

8. Place spinach (⅛ portion each) on each of the 8 laver sheets.

Seasoning the Cooked Rice

In a large bowl, stir the rice seasoning ingredients until the sugar and salt dissolve, then add the cooked rice, mix, and let cool slightly.

Rolling the Kimbap

Place the cooked rice (¼ portion) on 1 laver sheet from ③.

↓

↓

Place 2 spinach rolls from ⑧ on top, spacing them apart.

↓

Place 1 egg bacon roll from ⑦ between the spinach rolls and roll up.

↓

Make 3 more rolls and cut into bite-sized pieces.

Kabocha Squash & Tteokgalbi Kimbap

This kimbap is made with sweet and soft kabocha squash salad and savory *tteokgalbi*, which everyone loves. The dish is lavishly complemented with minced nuts for an extra crunchy texture.

⏱ **35–45 minutes / 2 rolls (1 roll = 410 kcal)**
- 1 bowl (200 g) warm rice
- 2 laver sheets
- 1 store-bought *tteokgalbi* (75 g)
- ¼ cucumber
- 4 lettuce leaves (palm size)
- a pinch of salt
- 1 Tbsp cooking oil

Kabocha Squash Salad
- ⅓ (270 g) kabocha squash
- 5 Tbsp (50 g) minced nuts (optional)
- 1 Tbsp mayonnaise (or plain yogurt)
- ½ Tbsp honey mustard
- 2 Tbsp oligofructose
- a pinch of salt

Tteokgalbi Seasoning
- 1 Tbsp brewed soy sauce
- 2 tsp sugar
- 1 tsp oligofructose

Cooked Rice Seasoning
- 2 tsp sesame seeds
- ⅓ tsp salt
- 2 tsp sesame oil

Preparing the Ingredients

1. **Kabocha squash** Scrape out the seeds with a spoon, place in a heatproof container, cover, and microwave (700W) for 5 minutes to fully cook. Use a spoon to scoop out the flesh.

2. **Cucumber** Remove seeds, finely shred, toss with salt, and let sit for 10 minutes. Drain in a sieve and rinse under cold water, then wrap in a paper towel to drain (see page 25).

3. **Lettuce** Wash under running water and shake off the water.
   Tteokgalbi Slice into 2×10 cm pieces.

4. In a bowl, combine the kabocha squash salad ingredients. In another bowl, combine the ingredients for the *tteokgalbi* seasoning.

5. Add cooking oil to a hot pan, add *tteokgalbi*, and cook over medium-low heat for 1 minute each side, then add *tteokgalbi* seasoning and cook, turning, for 2 minutes.

Seasoning the Cooked Rice

In a large bowl, mix the cooked rice and the seasoning ingredients, then let cool slightly.

Substitute Kabocha Squash

You can replace the kabocha squash with an equal amount of sweet potato, or use store-bought kabocha squash salad or sweet potato salad. In this case, skip step ①.

Rolling the Kimbap

Spread the cooked rice (½ portion) ¾ of the way across the laver.

↓

Spread 2 pieces of lettuce and top with the kabocha squash salad (½ portion) to wrap it with lettuce.

↓

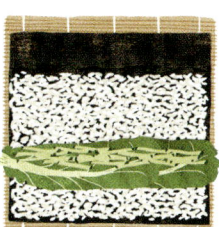

Top with shredded cucumber (½ portion).

↓

Top with *tteokgalbi* (½ portion) and roll up.

↓

Make 1 more roll and cut into bite-sized pieces.

Smiley Kimbap

The cute smile on this kimbap is sure to capture your heart. The cooked rice is seasoned with *furikake* to add flavor. A little attention to the placement of the rice and hot dog/sausage will help you create a cute look to your kimbap.

25–35 minutes / 3 rolls (1 roll = 289 kcal)
- 1½ bowls (300 g) warm rice
- 3 laver sheets
- 3 hot dogs/sausages (180 g)
- 1 tsp cooking oil

Cooked Rice Seasoning
- 1½ tsp *furikake* (or 2 tsp sesame seeds + ¼ tsp salt + 2 tsp sesame oil)

Garnishes
- black sesame seeds
- a dash of ketchup

Preparing the Ingredients

1. **Laver sheet** Remove ⅓ of a standard-sized laver sheet.

2. **Hot dog/Sausage** Cut into 2 lengthwise slices. Add cooking oil to a hot pan and cook 3 hot dogs/sausages over medium heat, turning, 1 minute.

Seasoning the Cooked Rice

In a large bowl, mix the cooked rice and the rice seasoning ingredients, then let cool slightly and divide into 9 equal portions.

Creating a Pouty Look

To create a pouty look, reverse the process shown on the right and place the hot dog/sausage with the cut side facing up. You can also create different looks by placing the black sesame seeds in different places.

Using Cut Laver

The laver you cut to make kimbap for kids can also be cut into thirds to make mini kimbap.

Rolling the Kimbap

Spread the cooked rice (2 portions) ¾ of the way across the laver.

↓

Top with more rice (1 portion) on the marked area.

↓

Top with the hot dog/sausage, cut side down, and roll up.

↓

Make 2 more rolls and cut into bite-sized pieces.

↓

Garnishing

Garnish with black sesame seeds and ketchup.

Smoked Duck Nude Kimbap

This type of kimbap is made with tender smoked duck, crispy vegetables, and sweet chili sauce. Different colored bell peppers add a nice vibrancy to the dish.

⏱ 25–35 minutes / 2 rolls (1 roll = 3.64 kcal)
- 1½ bowls (300 g) warm cooked rice
- 2 laver sheets
- 100 g sliced smoked duck
- ¼ cucumber (cut lengthwise)
- ¼ bell pepper
- 4 perilla leaves
- 2 Tbsp sweet chili sauce (or honey mustard)

Pickle Seasoning
- 1 Tbsp vinegar
- 2 tsp sugar
- a pinch of salt

Cooked Rice Seasoning
- 2 tsp black sesame seeds (or sesame seeds)
- ½ tsp salt
- 2 tsp sesame oil

Preparing the Ingredients

1. **Cucumber** Cut in half lengthwise and remove seeds. In a bowl, mix the pickle seasoning ingredients and marinate the cucumbers for 10 minutes, then squeeze out water (see page 25).

2. **Bell pepper** Shred.
   Perilla leaves Remove the stems.

3. Add the smoked duck to a hot pan and roast over medium heat for 2 minutes, then place the meat on a paper towel to remove oil.

Seasoning the Cooked Rice

In a large bowl, mix the cooked rice and the rice seasoning ingredients, then let cool slightly.

Substitute with Chicken Breast

You can also substitute the smoked duck with chicken breast (1 slice, 100 g), with the preparation process being the same.

Rolling the Kimbap

Wrap the entire kimbap roller in plastic wrap. Spread the rice so that it protrudes 0.5–1 cm beyond the end of the laver.

↓

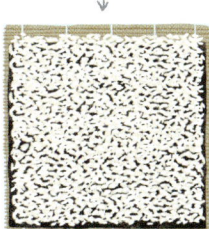

Flip the laver over so that the rice is facedown.

↓

Spread 2 perilla leaves, top with smoked duck (½ portion), and drizzle with 1 Tbsp sweet chili sauce.

↓

Top with shredded bell pepper (½ portion) and 1 strip of sliced cucumber, then roll up.

↓

Make 1 more roll and cut into bite-sized pieces.

Bassak Bulgogi & Water Parsley Kimbap

We've adapted a local dish from the Eonyang region, Korean *bassak* bulgogi, into kimbap. It's flavorful but not overly juicy, making it a perfect filling for kimbap. It also goes well with fragrant water parsley.

⏱ 30–40 minutes / 2 rolls (1 roll = 513 kcal)

- 1½ bowls (300 g) warm cooked rice
- 2 laver sheets
- 200 g beef for bulgogi (or minced beef)
- ½ fistful water parsley (35 g)
- 2 cheese slices (optional)
- ½ Tbsp cooking oil

Meat Seasoning

- 1½ Tbsp minced leek
- 1½ Tbsp brewed soy sauce
- ½ Tbsp cooking wine
- 4 tsp sugar
- ½ tsp minced garlic
- 1 tsp sesame oil

Cooked Rice Seasoning

- 2 tsp sesame seeds
- ½ tsp salt
- 2 tsp sesame oil

Preparing the Ingredients

1. **Beef** Wrap in a paper towel to remove blood, then pierce deeply with a sharp knife at 0.3 cm intervals. In a bowl, combine meat seasoning ingredients, beef, and toss to coat, then let sit for 10 minutes.
   ▶ This will tenderize the meat and marinate it well.

2. **Water parsley** Remove wilted leaves, wash under running water, drain, and cut into 2 or 3 pieces.
   Sliced cheese Cut into thirds and peel off the cover.

3. Add cooking oil to a hot pan and stir-fry the beef over high heat, turning with chopsticks, 3 minutes, then let cool slightly.

Seasoning the Cooked Rice

In a large bowl, mix the cooked rice and the rice seasoning ingredients, then let cool slightly.

Substitute with Other Vegetables

You can substitute the water parsley with 1 fistful (50 g) *chamnamul*, 1 fistful (50 g) garlic chives, or 10 perilla leaves. Perilla leaves should be rolled up and sliced.

Rolling the Kimbap

Spread the cooked rice (½ portion) ¾ of the way across the laver.

↓

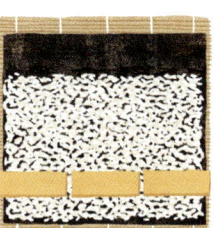

Top with sliced cheese (½ portion).

↓

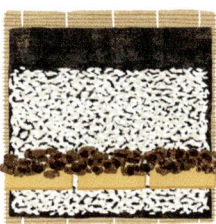

Top with *bassak* bulgogi (½ portion).

↓

Top with water parsley (½ portion) and roll up.

↓

Make 1 more roll and cut into bite-sized pieces.

Pork Cutlet Kimbap

This is a type of kimbap that combines thick pork cutlet with sweet and sour cabbage pickles. It was inspired by the fact that pork cutlets are usually served with cabbage pickles.

30–40 minutes / 2 rolls (1 roll = 649 kcal)

- 1½ bowls (300 g) warm cooked rice
- 2 laver sheets
- 2 sheets store-bought pork cutlet (200 g)
- 4 perilla leaves
- 3 cabbage leaves (palm size)
- 7 Tbsp cooking oil

Pickle Seasoning
- 1 Tbsp sugar
- 2 Tbsp vinegar
- ¼ tsp salt

Sesame Sauce
- 1½ Tbsp ground sesame seeds
- 1½ Tbsp pork cutlet sauce
- 1½ Tbsp mayonnaise

Cooked Rice Seasoning
- 2 tsp sesame seeds
- ¼ tsp salt
- 2 tsp sesame oil

Preparing the Ingredients

1. **Cabbage** Shred thinly, toss with pickle seasoning ingredients, and marinate for 10 minutes, then drain in a sieve.
Perilla leaves Remove the stems.

2. In a bowl, mix the sesame sauce ingredients.

3. Add cooking oil to a hot pan, add the pork cutlets, and prick them with a chopstick in 3 to 4 places. Roast over medium-low heat for 2 minutes, flip, and cook over low heat for 3 minutes and 30 seconds, then flip again and roast for 2 minutes.

4. Let the pork cutlets cool slightly on a paper towel, then slice into 3 cm wide pieces.

Seasoning the Cooked Rice

In a large bowl, mix the cooked rice and the rice seasoning ingredients, then let cool slightly.

Using Deep-Fried Shrimp

You can substitute deep-fried shrimp for the pork cutlets. It's also nice to use 4 store-bought fried shrimp for the kimbap and serve with sweet chili sauce or tartar sauce.

Tartar Sauce
1 Tbsp minced onion + 4 Tbsp mayonnaise + ½ Tbsp oligofructose + ¼ tsp salt + ½ tsp mustard + a pinch of ground black pepper

Rolling the Kimbap

Spread the cooked rice (½ portion) ¾ of the way across the laver.

↓

Spread sesame sauce (½ portion) evenly on 2 perilla leaves.

↓

Top with pork cutlet (½ portion).

↓

Top with pickled cabbage (½ portion) and roll up.

↓

Make 1 more roll and cut into bite-sized pieces.

Omelet Rice Kimbap

This kimbap is an adaptation of omelet rice, where stir-fried rice is wrapped in an egg crepe and drizzled with ketchup. The cooked rice is seasoned with ketchup, but you can also use whatever vegetables you have on hand.

⏱ **30–40 minutes / 3 rolls (1 roll = 304 kcal)**
- 1½ bowls (300 g) warm cooked rice
- 3 laver sheets
- ¼ potato
- ½ bell pepper
- 50 g ham
- 2 eggs
- a pinch of salt
- 2 tsp oyster sauce (add or subtract as desired)
- 1 tsp + 1 Tbsp cooking oil

Cooked Rice Seasoning
- 3 Tbsp ketchup
- ¼ tsp salt (add or subtract as desired)

Preparing the Ingredients

1. **Ham** Slice into 0.7 cm thick slices.
   Potatoes and bell pepper Slice into 0.5 cm thick slices.
   Eggs Whisk eggs and salt in a bowl.

2. Add cooking oil (1 tsp) to a hot pan and spread evenly with a paper towel. Pour in the egg wash and cook over low heat for 1 minute, flip, remove from heat, and let sit for 1 minute. Let it cool slightly and shape into three 20×8 cm square egg crepe.

3. Wipe the pan clean with a paper towel and heat the pan, add cooking oil (1 Tbsp), and stir-fry the potato over medium heat for 2 minutes, then add the bell pepper, ham, and oyster sauce to stir-fry for 1 minute.

Seasoning the Cooked Rice

In a large bowl, mix the cooked rice and the rice seasoning ingredients, then let cool slightly.

Rolling the Kimbap

Spread the cooked rice (⅓ portion) ¾ of the way across the laver.

↓

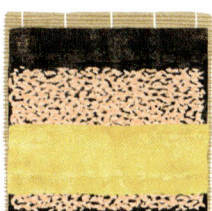

Top with egg crepe.

↓

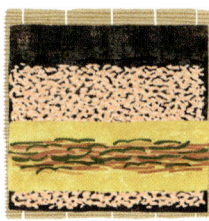

Top with the stir fry from ③ (⅓ portion) and roll up.

↓

Make 2 more rolls and cut into bite-sized pieces.

Make It Scrambled Eggs

Instead of making an egg crepe and wrapping it, you can also use scrambled eggs. Pour in the egg wash from step ② and cook over medium heat for 1 minute, stirring with chopsticks. Follow the same steps the rest of the way.

Avocado & Crab Meat Kimbap

This type of fusion kimbap is made with soft, savory avocado and crab meat. The salty crab meat is seasoned with mayonnaise and honey mustard, while the sweet and sour yellow pickled radish adds texture.

⏱ 40–50 minutes / 2 rolls (1 roll = 559 kcal)
- 1½ bowls (300 g) warm cooked rice
- 2 laver sheets
- ¼ avocado
- 8 pieces crab meat (small pieces)
- 3 eggs
- ¼ cucumber
- 2 strips yellow pickled radish
- a pinch of salt
- 1 tsp cooking oil
- a little lemon juice
- 2 Tbsp flying fish roe (optional)

Crab Meat Seasoning
- 1 Tbsp mayonnaise
- 1 Tbsp mustard
- ⅓ tsp sugar
- a pinch of salt
- a little lemon juice

Cooked Rice Seasoning
- 1 Tbsp sesame seeds
- 1 Tbsp vinegar
- 2 tsp sugar
- ⅓ tsp salt

Preparing the Ingredients

1. **Cucumber** Remove seeds and shred finely (see page 25).
2. **Crab meat** Tear it up into small pieces and mix it with the crab meat seasoning ingredients (see page 27).
   Yellow pickled radish Rinse under running water and remove any leftover water.
   Eggs In a bowl, whisk the eggs and a pinch of salt.
3. See page 28 to make chunky egg strips.
4. While the egg is still hot, place it on a kimbap roller and press firmly to shape. Let cool slightly and cut into 1 cm wide slices.
5. **Avocado** Prepare (see page 12), shred finely, and sprinkle with lemon juice.
   ▶ The lemon juice prevents the avocado from changing color.

Seasoning the Cooked Rice

In a large bowl, stir the rice seasoning ingredients until the sugar and salt dissolve, then add the cooked rice, mix, and let cool slightly.

Using Avocados

Unripe avocados can be stored unpeeled at room temperature for 2–3 days or in a rice bin to speed up ripening. For leftover avocados, brush the flesh with lemon juice to prevent browning, wrap in plastic wrap, and refrigerate (5–7 days).

Rolling the Kimbap

Wrap the kimbap roller in plastic wrap. Spread the cooked rice (½ portion) to 0.5–1 cm above the end of the laver. Flip the laver over.

↓

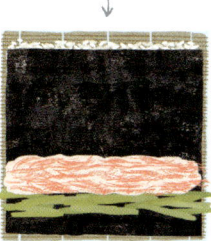

Top with shredded avocado (½ portion) and crab meat (½ portion).

↓

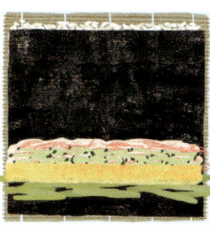

Top with shredded cucumber (½ portion) and 1 egg strip.

↓

Top with 1 strip yellow pickled radish and roll up. Spread the flying fish roe in a large bowl and roll the kimbap.

↓

Make 1 more roll and cut into bite-sized pieces.

Teriyaki Shrimp Kimbap

Chewy shrimp and crunchy cabbage are stir-fried in a sweet and salty teriyaki seasoning. Fillings for this kimbap are easy to prepare in one quick stir-fry.

30–40 minutes / 3 rolls (1 roll = 313 kcal)
- 1½ bowls (300 g) warm cooked rice
- 3 laver sheets
- 15 frozen raw shrimp (king size, 225 g)
- 5 cabbage leaves (palm size)
- 1 Tbsp cooking oil

Cooked Rice Seasoning
- 2 tsp sesame seeds
- ½ tsp salt
- 2 tsp sesame oil

Seasoning
- 2½ Tbsp brewed soy sauce
- 2 Tbsp cooking wine
- 1 Tbsp oligofructose
- ½ tsp sugar
- a pinch of ground black pepper

Preparing the Ingredients

1. **Frozen raw shrimp meat** Soak in water (2 cups) for 10 minutes to thaw. Place in a sieve and rinse under cold water, drain, and cut each shrimp into 2 pieces.
   Cabbage Shred finely.

2. In a small bowl, mix the seasoning ingredients.

3. Add cooking oil to a hot pan, add shrimp and stir-fry over high heat for 1 minute, add seasoning from ②, reduce heat to medium, and stir-fry for 3 minutes, then add cabbage and stir-fry for 1 minute.

Seasoning the Cooked Rice

In a large bowl, mix the cooked rice and the rice seasoning ingredients, then let cool slightly.

Rolling the Kimbap

Spread the cooked rice (⅓ portion) ¾ of the way across the laver.

↓

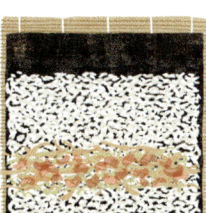

Top with stir-fried shrimp & cabbage (⅓ portion) and roll up.

↓

Make 2 more rolls and cut into bite-sized pieces.

Substitute with Chicken Tenderloin

It's also nice to use chicken tenderloin in place of shrimp. Remove the tendons from 6 chicken tenderloins, cut each lengthwise into 2 pieces, toss with ⅓ tsp salt and 2 tsp cooking wine, let sit for 10 minutes, and stir-fry in step ③.

Enjoy It Spicy

You can also add 1 sliced Cheongyang chili pepper to the seasoning ingredients.

Sprout Salad & Tuna Kimbap

Canned tuna, which is readily available in supermarkets, is a popular ingredient for kimbap, but this recipe uses sprouts, which have just a hint of a tangy flavor, to remove the oily taste, and minced pickles for a crunchy texture.

⏱ 20–30 minutes / 3 rolls (1 roll = 303 kcal)
- 1½ bowls (300 g) warm cooked rice
- 3 laver sheets
- 2 fistfuls sprouts (50 g)
- 1 canned tuna (150 g)
- 3 pickles (or 2 strips yellow pickled radish, 90 g)

Tuna Seasoning
- 2½ Tbsp mayonnaise
- ¼ tsp ground black pepper
- 1 tsp vinegar

Cooked Rice Seasoning
- ½ tsp salt
- 1 tsp sesame oil

Preparing the Ingredients

1. **Sprouts** Place in a sieve and rinse under running water.
2. **Tuna** Place in a sieve and press with a spoon to remove oil.
3. **Pickles** Finely mince and press dry with a paper towel.
4. In a bowl, mix the tuna, pickles, and tuna seasoning ingredients together well.

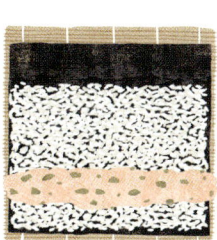

Seasoning the Cooked Rice

In a large bowl, mix the cooked rice and the rice seasoning ingredients, then let cool slightly.

Rolling the Kimbap

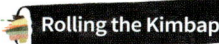

Spread the cooked rice (⅓ portion) ¾ of the way across the laver.

↓

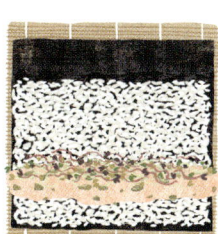

Top with tuna from ④ (⅓ portion).

↓

Top with sprouts (⅓ portion) and roll up.

↓

Make 2 more rolls and cut into bite-sized pieces.

Using Young Leafy Greens

Young leafy greens are a great substitute for sprouts, as they have a slightly tangy flavor.

Eel Kimbap

This is a premium type of kimbap that is easily made using store-bought grilled eel. The eel is flavored with pickled ginger to remove any unpleasant fishy smell, while radish sprouts are used to remove any oily flavor. Homemade eel kimbap can be just as good as any from a high-end kimbap restaurant.

⏱ **25–35 minutes / 2 rolls (1 roll = 656 kcal)**

- 1½ bowls (300 g) warm cooked rice
- 2 laver sheets
- 2 store-bought grilled eel (200 g)
- 3 eggs
- 20 g pickled ginger (add or subtract as desired)
- 1 fistful radish sprouts
- a pinch of salt
- 1 Tbsp cooking oil

Cooked Rice Seasoning
- 1 Tbsp vinegar
- 2 tsp sugar
- ⅓ tsp salt

Preparing the Ingredients

1. **Radish sprouts** Wash in cold water and drain in a sieve.
   Pickled ginger Drain in a sieve.
   Eggs In a bowl, whisk together the eggs and salt.

2. See page 28 to make chunky egg strips.

3. While the egg roll is still hot, place it on a kimbap roller and press firmly to shape. Let cool slightly and slice into 1 cm wide strips.

4. **Grilled eel** Add cooking oil (2 tsp) to a hot pan, place eel flesh side down, and grill over medium-low heat for 3 minutes, turning.
   ▶ Be careful to control the heat, as the sauce is easy to burn.

Seasoning the Cooked Rice

In a large bowl, stir the rice seasoning ingredients until the sugar and salt dissolve, then add the cooked rice, mix, and let cool slightly.

Making Braised Eel

Homemade braised eel preserves the seasoning well and tastes great. Use 2 eels (200 g) and 1 dried chili pepper + 2 garlic cloves + 1 ginger root + 5 Tbsp cooking wine + 4½ Tbsp brewed soy sauce + 3 Tbsp oligofructose + 2 tsp sugar + 1 tsp peppercorns + ⅖ cup water (100 ml). Bring to a boil over high heat, reduce heat, and cook for 10 minutes, while adding seasoning over the eel. Remove the eel to use in kimbap.

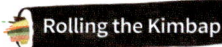
Rolling the Kimbap

Spread the cooked rice (½ portion) ¾ of the way across the laver.

↓

Top with 1 grilled eel and radish sprouts (½ portion).

↓

Top with pickled ginger (½ portion).

↓

Top with 1 strip egg roll and roll up.

↓

Make 1 more roll and cut into bite-sized pieces.
▶ This goes well with mayonnaise.

Salmon Kimbap

This type of kimbap is made with tender smoked salmon and crunchy apple, which goes well with the salmon. Instead of yellow pickled radish, sweet and sour onion pickles are used and flavored with minced garlic and prepared wasabi.

⏱ **30–40 minutes / 2 rolls (1 roll = 504 kcal)**
- 1½ bowls (300 g) warm cooked rice
- 2 laver sheets
- 4 strips of smoked salmon (100 g)
- ½ onion
- ½ apple
- 40 g sprouts (optional)
- 4 lettuce leaves

Onion Seasoning
- 2 Tbsp sugar
- 3 Tbsp vinegar
- a pinch of salt

Mayonnaise Mixture
- 3 Tbsp mayonnaise
- 2 tsp grated Parmesan cheese
- 2 tsp sugar
- 1 tsp minced garlic
- 1 tsp lemon juice (or vinegar)
- ½ tsp prepared wasabi

Cooked Rice Seasoning
- 1 Tbsp vinegar
- 2 tsp sugar
- ⅓ tsp salt

Preparing the Ingredients

1. **Onion** Cut into 0.5 cm thick slices, toss with the onion seasoning, and let sit for 20 minutes, then drain in a sieve.

2. **Apple** Cut into 0.5 cm thick slices.
   ▶ You can also soak shredded apple in sugar water to prevent it from browning if left out for too long after shredding.

3. **Sprout vegetables** Wash under running water and drain in a sieve. Wrap in paper towels to remove as much water as possible.
   Lettuce Wash under running water and shake off the water.

4. In a bowl, whisk together the mayonnaise mixture ingredients.

Seasoning the Cooked Rice

In a large bowl, stir the rice seasoning ingredients until the sugar and salt dissolve, then add the cooked rice, mix, and let cool slightly.

Enjoy as Salmon Rolls

When rolling the kimbap, omit the smoked salmon from the fillings and roll it into nude kimbap with thick egg strips or crab meat. Cut the salmon into 1 cm thick slices, place on the nude kimbap, wrap in plastic wrap to secure, and cut into bite-sized pieces. This allows you to enjoy kimbap with a different look.

Rolling the Kimbap

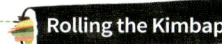

Spread the cooked rice (½ portion) ¾ of the way across the laver.

↓

Spread 2 lettuce leaves and place mayonnaise mixture (½ portion) in the center.

↓

Place smoked salmon in 2 layers and top with onion pickles (½ portion).

↓

Top with shredded apple (½ portion) and sprout vegetables (½ portion), then roll up.

↓

Make 1 more roll and cut into bite-sized pieces.

Cucumber Cream Cheese Nude Kimbap

Relatively easy to make and done so without the use of heat, this nude kimbap has a fun texture featuring flying fish roe popping out from the cream cheese.

25–35 minutes / 3 rolls (1 roll = 308 kcal)
- 1½ bowls (300 g) warm cooked rice
- 3 laver sheets
- 1 cucumber (200 g)
- 1 Tbsp flying fish roe (optional)
- 1½ Tbsp cream cheese at room temperature

Pickle Seasoning
- 1⅓ Tbsp sugar
- 2 Tbsp vinegar
- 1 tsp salt

Cooked Rice Seasoning
- 3 Tbsp water from pickled cucumber (or 1 Tbsp sugar + ½ Tbsp vinegar)
- 2 tsp sesame seeds
- ½ tsp salt

Preparing the Ingredients

1. **Laver sheet** Remove ⅓ of a standard-size laver sheet.
   Cucumber Remove seeds and finely shred (see page 25).

2. In a bowl, combine the cucumber and pickle seasoning ingredients, toss, and let sit for 5 minutes, then squeeze out the water.
   ▶ Set aside the water from the squeezed cucumber and use it to season the cooked rice.

3. Toss the cucumber with the flying fish roe and cream cheese.

Seasoning the Cooked Rice

In a large bowl, combine the water from the pickled cucumber from ②, sesame seeds, and salt to dissolve completely, then add the cooked rice and mix before letting it cool slightly.

Rolling the Kimbap

Wrap the kimbap roller in plastic wrap. Spread the cooked rice (⅓ portion) to 0.5–1 cm above the end of the laver.

↓

Flip the laver over so that the rice is facedown.

↓

Top with ⅓ of the cucumber cream cheese filling and roll the kimbap.

↓

Make 2 more rolls and cut into bite-sized pieces.

Enjoy It Spicy

You can also finely mince 2 chili peppers and mix them in with the flying fish roe and cream cheese in step ③.

Pollock Roe Kimbap

This is a type of kimbap where you can really taste the unique flavor of salted pollock roe. The soft egg and cucumber tossed with mayonnaise go well with the salty flavor of the salted pollock roe.

⏱ **30–40 minutes / 2 rolls (1 roll = 511 kcal)**
- 1½ bowls (300 g) warm cooked rice
- 2 laver sheets
- 2 portions salted pollock roe (120 g)
- 2 eggs
- ½ cucumber
- 2 Tbsp mayonnaise
- 1 tsp cooking oil
- ½ tsp salt

Salted Pollock Roe Seasoning
- 1 tsp sesame seeds
- 1 tsp sesame oil

Cooked Rice Seasoning
- 2 tsp sesame seeds
- ¼ tsp salt
- 2 tsp sesame oil

Preparing the Ingredients

1. **Cucumber** Peel, seed, and finely shred; toss with salt (¼ tsp) and let sit for 10 minutes. Drain in a sieve and rinse under cold water, then wrap in a paper towel to drain (see page 25).
In a bowl, toss the cucumber and mayonnaise.

2. **Salted pollock roe** Rinse off the existing seasoning and insert a knife into the length of the roe. Take the roe out with the blade. In a bowl, toss the pollock roe and the seasoning ingredients.

3. **Eggs** In a bowl, whisk eggs and salt (¼ tsp). Add cooking oil to a hot pan, spread evenly with a paper towel, pour in the egg wash and cook over low heat for 1 minute, then flip and cook for 30 seconds. Let cool slightly and finely shred.

Seasoning the Cooked Rice

In a large bowl, mix the cooked rice and the rice seasoning ingredients, then let cool slightly.

Enjoy It Spicy

You can also spice things up by adding 1 tsp red pepper powder to the pollock roe seasoning ingredients.

Rolling the Kimbap

Spread the cooked rice (½ portion) ¾ of the way across the laver.

↓

Top with shredded egg (½ portion).

↓

Top with seasoned pollock roe (½ portion).

↓

Top with shredded cucumber (½ portion) and roll up.

↓

Make 1 more roll and cut into bite-sized pieces.

Namul Kimbap

This type of kimbap is full of a *namul* fragrance. The colors of the three ingredients—*chwinamul* (aster scaber), egg, and carrot—blend well together, helping make it look and taste delicious. To enhance the texture of *chwinamul*, the egg and carrot should be shredded.

35–45 minutes / 2 rolls (1 roll = 506 kcal)

- 1½ bowls (300 g) warm cooked rice
- 2 laver sheets
- 25 g dried *chwinamul* (after soaking 100 g)
- ½ carrot
- 2 eggs
- 2 strips yellow pickled radish
- 2 tsp + 1 Tbsp cooking oil
- a pinch of salt + ⅓ tsp salt
- 1 Tbsp perilla powder
- 1 Tbsp perilla oil (or sesame oil)

Chwinamul Seasoning

- 1 Tbsp minced leek
- 1 tsp minced garlic
- 1½ tsp soy sauce for soup

Cooked Rice Seasoning

- 2 tsp sesame seeds
- ½ tsp salt
- 2 tsp sesame oil

Preparing the Ingredients

1. **Carrot** Shred.
   Eggs In a bowl, whisk the eggs and a pinch of salt.
2. See page 29 to make shredded egg.
3. Wipe the pan clean with a paper towel, add cooking oil, and stir-fry carrot and salt over medium-low heat for 2 minutes, then set aside.
4. In a bowl, toss the *chwinamul* and *chwinamul* seasoning. Add cooking oil (1 Tbsp) to a hot pan, add *chwinamul*, and stir-fry over medium-low heat for 5 minutes.
5. Turn off the heat and add the perilla powder and perilla oil, then stir-fry over the remaining heat as it cools down.

Seasoning the Cooked Rice

In a large bowl, mix the cooked rice and the rice seasoning ingredients, then let cool slightly.

Soaking Chwinamul

Cover dried *chwinamul* (25 g) with enough water to submerge and soak for 8 hours, then rinse several times. Place the *chwinamul* and water (4 cups) in a saucepan, bring to a boil, and cook over medium heat for 25 minutes. Soak the cooked *chwinamul* in cold water for 30 minutes to remove its characteristic odor, remove tough or spoiled leaves, and squeeze out water.

Rolling the Kimbap

Wrap the kimbap roller in plastic wrap. Spread the cooked rice (½ portion) to 0.5–1 cm above the end of the laver. Flip the laver over so that the rice is facedown.

↓

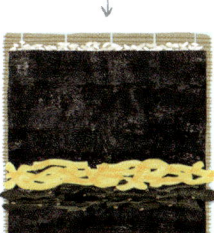

Top with *chwinamul* (½ portion) and shredded egg strips (½ portion).

↓

Top with shredded carrot (½ portion).

↓

Top with 1 strip yellow pickled radish and roll up.

↓

Make 1 more roll and cut into bite-sized pieces.

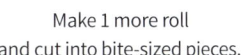

Addictive Kimbap

This is a specialty kimbap called "addictive kimbap" from Seoul's Gwangjang Market because of how addictive it is when dipped in the sauce. Enjoy the two sauces according to your taste.

⏲ 25–35 minutes / 18 pieces (1 piece = 36 kcal)
- 1½ bowls (300 g) cooked rice
- 3 laver sheets
- ½ carrot (100 g)
- 3 strips yellow pickled radish
- 1 tsp cooking oil
- ⅓ tsp salt

Cooked Rice Seasoning
- ⅔ Tbsp sesame oil
- 2 tsp sesame seeds
- ½ tsp salt

Sauce 1. Chili Pepper Sauce
- 1 green chili pepper, diced
- 1 Tbsp hot sauce
- 1 tsp brewed soy sauce
- 1 tsp oligofructose
- 1 tsp sesame oil

Sauce 2. Mustard
- 1 Tbsp water
- 1 Tbsp brewed soy sauce
- 1½ tsp sugar
- 1 tsp vinegar
- 1 tsp mustard

Preparing the Ingredients

1. **Laver sheet** Remove ⅓ of a standard-sized laver sheet.
   Carrot Thinly shred.
   Yellow pickled radish Place in a sieve and rinse under running water, then drain.
2. Make the desired sauce according to your taste.
3. Add cooking oil to a hot pan and stir-fry the carrot and salt over medium heat for 1 minute.

Seasoning the Cooked Rice

In a large bowl, mix the cooked rice and the rice seasoning ingredients, then let cool slightly.

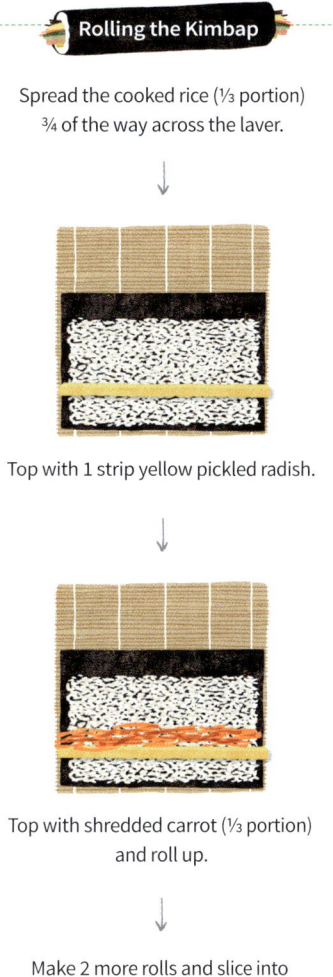

Rolling the Kimbap

Spread the cooked rice (⅓ portion) ¾ of the way across the laver.

↓

Top with 1 strip yellow pickled radish.

↓

Top with shredded carrot (⅓ portion) and roll up.

↓

Make 2 more rolls and slice into 3 cm wide pieces. Serve with sauce.

Enjoy Namdaemun-Style Mini Kimbap

Add the seasoned spinach (see page 24) to roll mini kimbap. Omit the sauce. Evenly apply the kimbap with sesame oil and sesame seeds for a savory Namdaemun-style kimbap.

Buckwheat Kimbap

This is an unusual type of kimbap made with buckwheat noodles instead of cooked rice. The buckwheat noodles are flavored with soy sauce, sugar, and sesame oil, while bell pepper, apple, cucumber, and radish are added for a crunchy texture and refreshing taste.

⏱ **35–45 minutes / 2 rolls (1 roll = 283 kcal)**
- 1 fistful dry buckwheat noodles (or thin noodles, 70 g)
- 2 laver sheets
- ¼ bell pepper
- ¼ apple
- ⅓ cucumber
- 2 eggs
- 8 slices store-bought *ssammu*
- a pinch of salt

Wasabi Soy Sauce
- 1 Tbsp water
- 1 Tbsp brewed soy sauce
- 1 Tbsp sesame oil
- 1 tsp sugar
- 1 tsp vinegar
- ½ tsp prepared wasabi

Base Seasoning
- 1 Tbsp sesame oil
- ½ tsp sugar
- 2 tsp brewed soy sauce

Preparing the Ingredients

1. **Cucumber** Remove seeds and shred finely (see page 25).

2. **Bell pepper** Shred.
   Ssammu Squeeze out water.
   Eggs In a bowl, whisk the eggs and a pinch of salt.

3. See page 29 to make shredded egg.

4. **Apple** Cut into 0.5 cm thick slices.
   ▶ You can also soak shredded apple in sugar water to prevent it from browning if left out for too long after shredding.

5. In a small bowl, mix the wasabi soy sauce ingredients.

Seasoning Noodles

Cook buckwheat noodles in boiling water (4 cups), rinse under cold water, drain, and toss with the base seasoning ingredients.
▶ Cook the noodles for the number of minutes according to package directions.

Enjoy as Cold Buckwheat Kimbap

It's also nice to place the seasoned noodles in the refrigerator for 10 minutes before making kimbap.

Enjoy as Vietnamese Spring Rolls

Soak 4 rice papers in warm water, spread them, and wrap the finished cold buckwheat kimbap. Serve with sweet chili sauce according to your taste.

Rolling the Kimbap

Spread the buckwheat noodles (½ portion) ¾ of the way across the laver.
↓

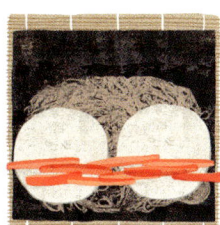

Spread 4 *ssammu* slices and top with shredded bell pepper (½ portion).
↓

Top with shredded apple (½ portion) and cucumber (½ portion).
↓

Top with shredded egg strips (½ portion) and roll up.
↓

Make 1 more roll and cut into bite-sized pieces.

Make It Extra Special

Perfect Side Dishes for a Kimbap Lunch Box

When packing a picnic lunch, include these cute side dishes that kids will love!

Octopus Sausage
- 4–5 Vienna sausages
- 1 tsp cooking oil
- a pinch of black sesame seeds

❶ Slice the Vienna sausages into cross (+) slices ⅔ of the way through.

❷ Add cooking oil to a hot pan, add Vienna sausages, and stir-fry over medium heat for 2 minutes.

❸ Let them cool slightly and garnish with black sesame seeds.

Quail Egg Chick (Yellow/Pink)
- 20 quail eggs (or hard-boiled ones)
- a pinch of black sesame seeds
- 1 slice carrot
- 2 cups (500 ml) water
- 2 Tbsp curry powder
- 15 g beets

❶ Place the quail eggs, a pinch of salt, and enough water to cover them in a saucepan. Bring to a boil over high heat, then reduce heat to medium-low and simmer for 10 minutes.

❷ Place in cold water to cool slightly and peel.

❸ **Beets (for pink)** Grate. In a bowl, combine 10 quail eggs, water (1 cup), and grated beets and soak for 3–4 hours.
Curry powder (for yellow) In a bowl, combine 10 quail eggs, water (1 cup), and curry powder, then soak for 1–2 hours.

❹ Garnish with black sesame seeds and tiny pieces of carrot.

CHAPTER 3

Slightly Spicy Kimbap

Most Koreans Don't Bat an Eyelash at This Level of Spiciness. :)

Seasoned Fried Chicken Kimbap

Crispy fried chicken tenderloin is tossed in a sweet and spicy seasoning. Crunchy yellow pickled radish adds texture, and the chicken is wrapped in lettuce to keep the chicken seasoning off the cooked rice.

50–60 minutes / 3 rolls (1 roll = 448 kcal)
- 1½ bowls (300 g) warm rice
- 3 laver sheets
- 6 chicken tenderloins (or chicken breasts, 150 g)
- 70 g crunchy yellow pickled radish (or 6 slices of *ssammu*)
- 6 lettuce leaves (palm size)
- 4 cups (1 ℓ) cooking oil

Base Seasoning
- 1 Tbsp cooking wine
- ⅓ tsp salt
- a pinch of freshly ground black pepper

Cooked Rice Seasoning
- 2 tsp sesame seeds
- ⅓ tsp salt
- 2 tsp sesame oil

Chicken Seasoning
- 3 Tbsp (30 g) minced peanuts
- 1½ Tbsp ketchup
- 1 Tbsp *gochujang*
- 3 Tbsp oligofructose
- 3 tsp sugar
- 1 tsp minced garlic
- 2 tsp brewed soy sauce

Fry Batter
- 5 Tbsp fry batter mix
- 2 Tbsp cooking oil
- ⅖ cup (100 ml) water

Preparing the Ingredients

1. **Chicken tenderloins** Remove tendons (see page 12) and cut into 2 lengthwise pieces. Toss with the base seasoning ingredients and let sit for 15 minutes.

2. **Crunchy yellow pickled radish** Squeeze dry.
   Lettuce Wash under running water and shake off the water.

3. Mix the chicken seasoning in a bowl. In another bowl, mix the fry batter ingredients with chopsticks, then add the chicken tenderloins and toss to coat.

4. Pour cooking oil into a thick pot and bring to a boil over medium heat to 150℃ (when you put the batter in, it should touch the bottom and float after 5 seconds). Add the chicken tenderloins from ③ one by one in long strips and fry for 3 minutes and 30 seconds, turning over, then drain in a sieve.

5. Heat the oil in ④ over high heat to 180℃ (when you add the batter, it goes down to the middle and rises after 2 seconds). Add ④ and fry over medium heat for 2 minutes until golden brown, then drain in a sieve to remove the oil.
   ▶ Fry twice to make them crispier.

6. Add chicken seasoning to a hot pan and boil for 30 seconds over medium-low heat, then add ⑤ and toss to coat for 2 minutes.

Seasoning the Cooked Rice

In a large bowl, mix the cooked rice and the rice seasoning ingredients, then let cool slightly.

Using Store-Bought Fried Chicken

If you have leftover fried chicken, you can use them for this kimbap. Add 1 tsp cooking oil to a hot pan and heat the chicken over low heat for 3 minutes, then let cool slightly before using.

Rolling the Kimbap

Spread the cooked rice (⅓ portion) ¾ of the way across the laver.

↓

Top with 2 pieces of lettuce.

↓

Top with seasoned fried chicken (⅓ portion).

↓

Top with crunchy yellow pickled radish (⅓ portion) and roll up.

↓

Make 2 more rolls and cut into bite-sized pieces.

Burger Kimbap

Reminiscent of a burger with its piled-up ingredients between cooked rice, this rectangular kimbap is filled with spicy grilled chicken tenderloin and plenty of veggies. Even one piece of this kimbap can make you feel full.

⏱ 35–45 minutes / 2 pieces (1 piece = 545 kcal)
- 1½ bowls (300 g) warm cooked rice
- 2 laver sheets
- 6 chicken tenderloins (or 1½ chicken thighs) 150 g
- ¼ onion
- 2 eggs
- 4 lettuce leaves (palm size)
- 4 perilla leaves
- 10 cm leek
- a pinch of salt
- 1 tsp + 1 Tbsp cooking oil

Cooked Rice Seasoning
- 2 tsp sesame seeds
- ½ tsp salt
- 2 tsp sesame oil

Base Seasoning for Chicken Tenderloins
- 1 Tbsp refined rice wine
- 2½ tsp sugar
- ½ tsp salt
- 1 tsp minced garlic
- a pinch of ground black pepper

Chicken Tenderloin Seasoning
- 1 Cheongyang chili pepper, minced
- 1 Tbsp water
- 1 Tbsp cooking wine
- 1½ Tbsp *gochujang*
- 1 tsp red pepper powder

Preparing the Ingredients

1. **Chicken tenderloins** Remove the tendons with a knife (see page 12) and cut into 2 cm pieces on all sides. Toss the tenderloins in the base seasoning.
   In another bowl, mix the chicken tenderloin seasoning.

2. **Lettuce** Wash under running water and shake off the water.
   Perilla leaves Remove stems.
   Onion Finely mince.
   Leek Chop into small pieces.
   Eggs In a bowl, whisk together the eggs and salt.

3. Add 1 tsp cooking oil to a hot pan, add the egg wash and cook over low heat for 1 minute, then flip and turn off the heat. Let sit for 1 minute and then form two 8×6 cm egg strips.

4. Reheat the pan, add 1 Tbsp cooking oil and stir-fry the chicken tenderloins, onion, and leek over medium heat for 3 minutes, then add the chicken tenderloin seasoning and stir-fry for 2 minutes.

Seasoning the Cooked Rice

In a large bowl, mix the cooked rice and the rice seasoning ingredients, then let cool slightly.

Enjoy with Curry Seasoning

You can also season the cooked rice with a mixture of 4 tsp curry powder + 1 tsp sugar + 3 tsp sesame seeds + 2 tsp olive oil (or grapeseed oil). Follow the same steps the rest of the way.

Rolling the Kimbap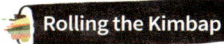

Spread the cooked rice (¼ portion) at the center of the laver.

↓

Top with 2 lettuce leaves → chicken tenderloin (½ portion).

↓

Place 2 perilla leaves on top of the egg strip (½ portion).

↓

↓

Top with the cooked rice (¼ portion) and wrap with the laver as shown above. Secure the completed kimbap with plastic wrap and cut into 2 pieces.

Garlic Chives & Bacon Kimbap

This type of kimbap is filled with salty bacon and tangy, seasoned garlic chives. These two ingredients alone are enough to satisfy your cravings, but it's important to remove as much of the bacon fat as possible so you can maximize the flavor.

⏱ **20–30 minutes / 3 rolls (1 roll = 300 kcal)**
- 1½ bowls (300 g) warm cooked rice
- 3 laver sheets
- 2 fistfuls garlic chives (100 g)
- 12 strips bacon

Cooked Rice Seasoning
- 2 tsp sesame seeds
- ½ tsp salt
- 2 tsp sesame oil

Garlic Chive Seasoning
- ½ Tbsp minced garlic
- ½ Tbsp vinegar
- ½ Tbsp oligofructose
- 2 tsp red pepper powder
- 2 tsp sesame seeds
- 1 tsp sesame oil
- a pinch of salt

Preparing the Ingredients

1. **Garlic chives** Cut into 2 pieces and lightly toss the garlic chives in the seasoning.
   - ▶ You can also blanch the garlic chives in boiling water for 3 seconds and then rinse them in cold water to reduce the pungency.

2. Add the bacon to the hot pan and cook over medium heat for 1 minute, each side, then wrap in paper towels to remove the fat.
   - ▶ Remove as much bacon fat as possible so that it doesn't taste greasy.

Seasoning the Cooked Rice

In a large bowl, mix the cooked rice and the rice seasoning ingredients, then let cool slightly.

Rolling the Kimbap

Spread the cooked rice (⅓ portion) ¾ of the way across the laver.

↓

Top with 4 strips of bacon.

↓

Top with garlic chives (⅓ portion) and roll up.

↓

Make 2 more rolls and cut into bite-sized pieces.

Substitute with Spinach

You can substitute garlic chives with an equal amount of spinach.
Add the spinach to boiling water (3 cups water + 1 tsp salt) and blanch for 30 seconds.
Rinse under cold water, squeeze out water, and toss with the seasoning ingredients from ①.
Follow the same steps the rest of the way.

Jeyuk Ssam Kimbap

A simple twist on a popular dish from a famous kimbap restaurant, this dish features deliciously seasoned, stir-fried pork wrapped in *gomchwi* leaves, which can also be substituted with cabbage or pumpkin leaves.

⏱ 30–40 minutes / 2 rolls (1 roll = 560 kcal)
- 1½ bowls (300 g) warm cooked rice
- 2 laver sheets
- pork for bulgogi (front or hind leg, 200 g)
- 4 perilla leaves (or lettuce)
- 8 store-bought *ssammu*
  (or 2 strips yellow pickled radish)
- 6 *gomchwi* leaves
  (or pumpkin leaves, cabbage, palm size, optional)
- 1 Tbsp cooking oil

Meat Seasoning
- ½ Tbsp sugar
- ½ Tbsp minced garlic
- ½ Tbsp brewed soy sauce
- 2 Tbsp *gochujang*
- 1 tsp sesame oil
- a pinch of ground black pepper

Cooked Rice Seasoning
- 2 tsp sesame seeds
- ¼ tsp salt
- 2 tsp sesame oil

Preparing the Ingredients

1. **Pork** Slice into 2 cm wide strips. In a bowl, combine the seasoning ingredients and pork, and toss to coat, then let sit for 10 minutes.

2. **Perilla leaves** Remove the stems.
   Ssammu Squeeze out water.

3. **Gomchwi** Remove stems and blanch in boiling water (4 cups water + 1 tsp salt) for 20 seconds, then rinse under cold water and squeeze out water.

4. Add cooking oil to a hot pan, add pork and stir-fry over medium heat, loosening with chopsticks, for 4 to 4.5 minutes.

Seasoning the Cooked Rice

In a large bowl, mix the cooked rice and the rice seasoning ingredients, then let cool slightly.

Enjoy It Non-spicy

You can make it non-spicy by replacing the meat seasoning ingredients with 1 Tbsp sugar + 1 Tbsp minced garlic + 2 Tbsp brewed soy sauce + 1 Tbsp refined rice wine + ½ Tbsp sesame oil + a pinch of black pepper.

Rolling the Kimbap

Wrap the kimbap roller in plastic wrap. Spread the cooked rice (½ portion) so that it protrudes 0.5–1 cm beyond the end of the laver. Flip the laver over so that the rice is facedown.

↓

Place 4 slices of *ssammu* and stir-fried pork (½ portion) on top of 2 perilla leaves.

↓

Wrap the ingredients with the perilla leaves first, then roll up.

↓

↓

Spread 3 slices of *gomchwi*, overlapping by 1 cm, and top with the kimbap to roll up tightly. Make 1 more roll and cut into bite-sized pieces.

Jangjorim Kimbap

This simple type of kimbap is made with a popular side dish, *jangjorim* (braised beef in soy sauce). The salty yet sweet *jangjorim* is cooled down with crunchy shredded cucumber, while the cooked rice is seasoned with butter, as it goes well with soy sauce for added flavor.

30–40 minutes / 2 rolls (1 roll = 327 kcal)
- 1½ bowls (300 g) warm cooked rice
- 2 laver sheets
- 80 g *jangjorim*
- ½ cucumber
- ¼ tsp salt

Cooked Rice Seasoning
- 1 Cheongyang chili pepper, minced
- 1½ Tbsp brewed soy sauce
- 3 tsp ground sesame seeds
- 2½ tsp sugar
- 2 tsp butter

Preparing the Ingredients

1. **Cucumber** Remove seeds and shred finely; toss with salt and let sit for 10 minutes. Drain in a sieve, rinse under cold water, and wrap in paper towels to remove any leftover water (see page 25).

2. **Jangjorim** Tear large pieces into small pieces by hand. Squeeze out the broth with your hands (see page 118).

Seasoning the Cooked Rice

In a large bowl, mix the cooked rice and the rice seasoning ingredients, then let cool slightly.
▶ You can also add 2 tsp butter to the *jangjorim* broth and use it as the cooked rice seasoning.

Rolling the Kimbap

Spread the cooked rice (½ portion) ¾ of the way across the laver.

↓

Top with *jangjorim* (½ portion).

↓

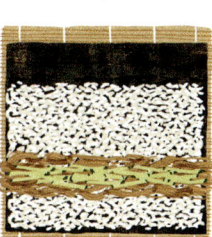

Top with shredded cucumber (½ portion).

↓

Make 1 more roll
and cut into bite-sized pieces.

Controlling the Saltiness

If the *jangjorim* is too salty, increase the amount of cucumber to ¾ or reduce the amount of *jangjorim* to 50 grams.

Substitute with Cucumber Pickles

You can also use cucumber pickles (50 grams) instead of cucumber.
Simply squeeze the water out of the pickles with your hands before shredding them.
Follow the same steps the rest of the way.

Seasoned Yellow Pickled Radish Kimbap

This type of kimbap is made with just yellow pickled radish, ham, and perilla leaves. It's not only delicious without any special ingredients, but it's also very simple to make, so you can put it together quickly when you're in a hurry. Seasoned yellow pickled radish is also great as a side dish.

⏱ 25–35 minutes / 2 rolls (1 roll = 297 kcal)
- 1½ bowls (300 g) warm cooked rice
- 2 laver sheets
- 100 g yellow pickled radish
  (diameter: 5 cm, length: 5 cm)
- 4 strips ham for kimbap
  (or other types of hot dog, sausage, or ham, 40 g)
- 4 perilla leaves (or other leafy vegetables)

Yellow Pickled Radish Seasoning
- 1 Tbsp red pepper powder
- 1 Tbsp minced leek
- 1 tsp sugar
- 1 tsp minced garlic
- ½ tsp brewed soy sauce
- 1 tsp sesame oil

Cooked Rice Seasoning
- 1 Tbsp sesame seeds
- 1 Tbsp sesame oil
- ½ tsp salt

Preparing the Ingredients

1. **Perilla leaves** Remove stems.
   Ham Blanch in boiling water for 1 minute, then drain in a sieve (see page 27).
   ▶ Blanching the ham will remove the fat and make it lighter.

2. **Yellow pickled radish** Shred into 0.5 cm thick slices and place in a sieve, rinse under running water. Wrap in paper towels to remove as much water as possible, then toss with the yellow pickled radish seasoning.

Seasoning the Cooked Rice

In a large bowl, mix the cooked rice and the rice seasoning ingredients, then let cool slightly.

Substitute with Tofu

You can also substitute ham with tofu. Prepare half a large package of tofu (150 g, firm) (see page 117). Add ½ Tbsp cooking oil to a hot pan and sear the tofu over medium heat for 2 minutes and 30 seconds on each side. Follow the same steps the rest of the way.

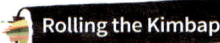

Rolling the Kimbap

Spread the cooked rice (½ portion) ¾ of the way across the laver.

↓

Spread 2 perilla leaves and top with 2 strips of ham.

↓

Top with yellow pickled radish (½ portion).

↓

Wrap the ingredients first with the perilla leaves and roll up.

↓

Make 1 more roll and cut into bite-sized pieces.

Spam Egg Roll

This type of kimbap is an adaptation of a popular menu item from a famous restaurant. The salty stir-fried ham & kimchi is wrapped in a soft egg crepe. It can be neatly sliced after the pizza cheese inside becomes slightly firm.

⏱ **30–40 minutes / 3 rolls (1 roll = 422 kcal)**
- 1½ bowls (300 g) warm cooked rice
- 3 laver sheets
- 100 g ripe napa cabbage kimchi
- 50 g canned ham
- 3 eggs
- 6 perilla leaves
- 100 g shredded pizza cheese (optional)
- a pinch of salt
- 2 tsp sesame oil
- 1 tsp sugar
- 3 tsp cooking oil

Cooked Rice Seasoning
- 1 Tbsp sesame seeds
- 1 Tbsp sesame oil
- a pinch of salt

Preparing the Ingredients

1. **Perilla leaves** Remove the stems.
   Shredded pizza cheese Finely mince.
   ▶ Finely mincing the pizza cheese prevents the surface from becoming lumpy when the kimbap is rolled in the egg.

2. **Canned ham** Shred into 0.5 cm thick slices.
   Napa cabbage kimchi Lightly shake off the seasoning, squeeze firmly with your hands, and thinly shred.
   Eggs Whisk eggs and salt in a bowl.
   ▶ If you want thicker, fluffier egg rolls, you can double the amount of eggs.

3. Add sesame oil to a hot pan, add kimchi, ham, and sugar, then stir-fry over medium heat for 2 minutes.

Seasoning the Cooked Rice

In a large bowl, mix the cooked rice and the rice seasoning ingredients, then let cool slightly.

Make Kimchi More Delicious

If using undercooked kimchi, add 1 tsp vinegar in step ③; if using overcooked kimchi, add 1 tsp sugar to the stir-fry.

Enjoy It Non-spicy

If your kimchi is too spicy, you can wash the napa cabbage kimchi under running water and squeeze the water out by hand before using.

Rolling the Kimbap

Spread the cooked rice (⅓ portion) ¾ of the way across the laver.

↓

↓

Spread 2 perilla leaves, top with stir-fried ham & kimchi from ③ (⅓ portion), and roll up. Make 2 more rolls.

↓

Rolling the eggs

Add 1 tsp cooking oil to a pan heated over low heat. Pour in the egg wash (⅓ portion) and tilt the pan to spread it across the pan.

↓

↓

When half cooked over low heat, sprinkle 4 Tbsp shredded pizza cheese evenly.

↓

↓

Place 1 kimbap roll on the edge of the egg and roll up with a spatula and chopsticks. Make 2 more rolls, let cool slightly, and cut into bite-sized pieces.

Dried Radish Strips Kimbap

This type of kimbap is made with seasoned dried radish strips, a side dish that tends to stay in the refrigerators of Koreans for a long time. It's a great combination of spicy and savory seasoned dried radish strips with a nice chewy texture, and blanched cabbage that is softened and subtly sweet.

⏱ **30–40 minutes / 2 rolls (1 roll = 347 kcal)**
- 1½ bowls (300 g) warm cooked rice
- 2 laver sheets
- 80 g seasoned dried radish strips
- 4 cabbage leaves (palm size, 120 g, optional)
- 4 strips of ham for kimbap (40 g)
- 1 tsp cooking oil

Cooked Rice Seasoning
- 2 tsp sesame seeds
- ½ tsp salt
- 2 tsp sesame oil

Preparing the Ingredients

1. **Cabbage** Blanch in boiling water (4 cups) + salt (1 tsp) for 5 minutes, then drain in a sieve and rinse under cold water. Wrap in paper towels to remove any leftover water.
   ▶ You can also cook the cabbage in the microwave (700W) for 5 minutes. In a heat-resistant container, combine cabbage and ½ cup (125 ml) water, then cover with plastic wrap.

2. Blanch ham in boiling water for 1 minute, then drain in a sieve. Add cooking oil to a hot pan and stir-fry over medium heat for 2 minutes.

Seasoning the Cooked Rice

In a large bowl, mix the cooked rice and the rice seasoning ingredients, then let cool slightly.

Reducing the Bitterness of Store-Bought Dried Radish Strips

If your dried radish strips are too bitter, wash them under running water, soak them in water (1 cup + 1 tsp sugar) for 10 minutes, squeeze them dry, and toss them in 1 Tbsp red pepper powder + ½ tsp sugar + ½ tsp minced garlic + 1 tsp oligofructose + 1 tsp *gochujang*.

Rolling the Kimbap

Wrap the kimbap roller in plastic wrap. Spread the cooked rice (½ portion) to 0.5–1 cm above the end of the laver. Flip the laver over so that the rice is facedown.

↓

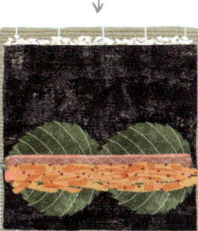

Spread 2 perilla leaves and top with seasoned dried radish strips (½ portion) and ham (½ portion).

↓

Wrap the ingredients with the perilla leaves and roll up.

↓

Spread 2 cabbage leaves, overlapping, and top with the kimbap to roll up tightly.

↓

Make 1 more roll and cut into bite-sized pieces.

Mukeunji Kimbap

The *mukeunji* (well-aged kimchi) lurking deep in your refrigerator can also serve as an ingredient for a delicious type of kimbap, with its deep sour flavor giving it a refreshing taste without the need for yellow pickled radish.

🕒 **40–50 minutes / 2 rolls (1 roll = 449 kcal)**
- 1½ bowls (300 g) warm cooked black rice (or white rice)
- 2 laver sheets
- 200 g *mukeunji*
- 2 fistfuls spinach (100 g)
- ⅓ carrot
- 2 eggs
- ½ sheet of rectangular fish cake
- 1 tsp salt + a pinch of salt
- 2 tsp sesame oil
- 2 tsp cooking oil

Mukeunji Seasoning
- 2 tsp sugar (add or subtract as desired)
- 2 tsp sesame oil

Cooked Rice Seasoning
- 2 tsp sesame seeds
- ½ tsp salt
- 2 tsp sesame oil

Preparing the Ingredients

1. **Spinach** Blanch in boiling water (3 cups water + 1 tsp salt) for 30 seconds, then rinse under cold water and squeeze out water. In a bowl, toss the spinach, salt (½ tsp), and sesame oil.

2. **Eggs** In a bowl, whisk the eggs and a pinch of salt.
   Mukeunji Rinse under running water and squeeze out water, then finely shred and toss with the *mukeunji* seasoning ingredients.
   Carrot Shred finely.
   Fish cake Cut into 2 cm wide strips.

3. See page 29 to make shredded egg.

4. Wipe the pan clean with a paper towel and reheat it, add cooking oil (1 tsp), and stir-fry the carrot and salt (½ tsp) over medium-low heat for 2 minutes and set aside.

5. Add the fish cake to the pan in ④ and stir-fry for 2 minutes over medium-low heat.

Seasoning the Cooked Rice

In a large bowl, mix the cooked rice and the rice seasoning ingredients, then let cool slightly.

Reducing the Sour Taste of Mukeunji

If *mukeunji* has a strong sour flavor, add 1 tsp sugar to the *mukeunji* seasoning ingredients. Follow the same steps the rest of the way.

Rolling the Kimbap

Spread the cooked rice (½ portion) ¾ of the way across the laver.

↓

Top with *mukeunji* (½ portion) and spinach (½ portion).

↓

Top with shredded carrot (½ portion) and shredded egg strips (½ portion).

↓

Top with fish cake (½ portion) and roll up.

↓

Make 1 more roll and cut into bite-sized pieces.

Dried Squid Strip Kimbap

Dried squid strips are a popular side dish because of their chewy texture and unique savory flavor. If you have leftover dried squid strips after making a side dish or have stir-fried dried squid strips in the refrigerator, try making kimbap using them. You can also add plenty of cool, fragrant cucumber.

⏱ 30–40 minutes / 2 rolls (1 roll = 439 kcal)
- 1½ bowls (300 g) warm cooked rice
- 2 laver sheets
- 100 g dried squid strips
- ½ cucumber
- 4 perilla leaves
- ¼ tsp salt

Dried Squid Strips Seasoning
- 1½ Tbsp *gochujang*
- 1 tsp sugar
- ½ tsp minced garlic
- ½ tsp mayonnaise
- 1 tsp oligofructose
- 1 tsp sesame oil

Cooked Rice Seasoning
- 2 tsp sesame seeds
- ½ tsp salt
- 2 tsp sesame oil

Preparing the Ingredients

1. **Dried squid strips** Cut into 4 cm lengths and soak in 2 cups (500 ml) of water for 5 minutes, then rinse under cold water and squeeze out water.
   ▶ You can also use stir-fried dried squid strips. Skip steps ①, ③, and ④ in that case.

2. **Cucumber** Remove the seeds and shred finely. Toss with salt and let sit for 10 minutes. Drain in a sieve, rinse under cold water, and wrap in paper towels to remove any leftover water (see page 25).
   Perilla leaves Remove stems.

3. In a small bowl, mix the dried squid strip seasoning ingredients.

4. Add the dried squid strips to a hot pan and stir-fry over medium heat for 2 minutes, then turn off the heat. Stir in the dried squid strip seasoning.

Seasoning the Cooked Rice

In a large bowl, mix the cooked rice and the rice seasoning ingredients, then let cool slightly.

Enjoy It Non-spicy

You can substitute the dried squid strip seasoning with soy sauce seasoning (1 Tbsp cooking wine + 1 tsp brewed soy sauce + 1 tsp mayonnaise + 1 tsp oligofructose). Follow the same steps the rest of the way.

Rolling the Kimbap

Spread the cooked rice (½ portion) ¾ of the way across the laver.

↓

Top with 2 perilla leaves.

↓

Top with stir-fried dried squid strips (½ portion).

↓

Top with cucumber (½ portion) and roll up.

↓

Make 1 more roll and cut into bite-sized pieces.

Chungmu Kimbap

Chungmu Kimbap is a popular dish from Tongyeong. This style of kimbap comes from the practice of serving kimbap and fillings separately to prevent the food from going bad, in consideration of those going out to sea. With their crunchy texture, radish kimchi and seasoned squid & fish cake also make great side dishes for simple cooked rice.

⏱ 30–40 minutes (+1 hour for pickling radish)
12 pieces (1 piece = 46 kcal), radish kimchi = 121 kcal, seasoned squid and fish cake = 505 kcal

- 1½ bowls (300 g) cooked rice
- 3 laver sheets
- 10 cm diameter, 3 cm thick radish (300 g)
- 1 squid (240 g, after prep 180 g)
- 2 rectangular fish cake sheets
- 15 cm leek

Radish Kimchi Seasoning
- 2 tsp red pepper powder
- ¼ tsp salt (add or subtract as desired)

For Salting Down Radish
- 2 Tbsp sugar
- 2½ Tbsp vinegar
- 1 tsp salt
- 1 tsp minced garlic

For Blanching the Squid
- 1 ginger root (garlic size)
- 1 Tbsp refined rice wine
- 3 cups water (750 ml)

Squid and Fish Cake Seasoning
- 2 Tbsp red pepper powder
- ½ Tbsp sugar
- 1 Tbsp brewed soy sauce
- 1 tsp minced garlic
- 1 tsp vinegar
- 1 tsp fish sauce (optional)
- 2 tsp sesame oil

Cooked Rice Seasoning
- 1 tsp sesame seeds
- ½ tsp salt
- 1 Tbsp sesame oil

Preparing the Ingredients

1. **Radish** Cross (+) quarter and cut into 1 cm thick slices. In a bowl, add seasoning for salting down radish and toss. After 1 hour, drain and toss with radish kimchi seasoning.
   ▶ Mix the radish while salting down.

2. **Laver** Cut into quarters.
   Leek Cut into 0.3 cm wide slices.
   Fish cake Cut into 1×4 cm pieces and blanch in boiling water for 1 minute, then drain.

3. **Squid** Prepare (see page 12). Cut a 0.5 cm wide slit on the inside, then cut into thirds and slice into 1 cm pieces, and cut the legs into 5 cm pieces.

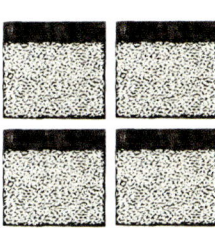

4. Combine the ingredients for blanching squid in a saucepan and bring to a boil, add the squid and blanch over high heat for 90 seconds, drain in a sieve and rinse under running water, then shake off the water.

5. Add the squid, fish cake, and leek to the seasoning ingredients and toss.

Seasoning the Cooked Rice

In a large bowl, mix the cooked rice and the rice seasoning ingredients, then let cool before dividing into thirds.

Rolling the Kimbap

Divide the cooked rice (⅓ portion) into quarters and spread ¾ of the way across the laver.

↓

Roll up.
Make 8 more rolls.

↓

Serve with radish kimchi and seasoned squid & fish cake.

Substitute with Octopus

Prepare the octopus and place in boiling water to blanch over high heat for 90 seconds, then slice into 5 cm lengths. Follow the same steps the rest of the way.

Tofu Kimchi Kimbap

This kimbap is inspired by a dish called tofu kimchi, which features blanched tofu wrapped in stir-fried kimchi. Instead of yellow pickled radish (a usual ingredient in kimbap), ripe kimchi is stir-fried making it sweet and sour. Grilling the tofu makes it a little easier to roll the kimbap.

⏱ 30–40 minutes / 2 rolls (1 roll = 464 kcal)
- 1½ bowls (300 g) warm cooked rice
- 2 laver sheets
- ½ large pack tofu (firm type, 150 g)
- 150 g ripe napa cabbage kimchi
- 4 perilla (or lettuce) leaves
- ⅓ tsp salt
- ½ Tbsp cooking oil

Tofu Seasoning
- ½ Tbsp sugar
- 1 Tbsp water
- 1 Tbsp brewed soy sauce

Cooked Rice Seasoning
- 1 Tbsp sesame seeds
- 1½ Tbsp sesame oil

Kimchi Seasoning
- 1 Tbsp sesame oil
- 1 tsp sugar
- 1 tsp red pepper powder

Preparing the Ingredients

1. **Tofu** Cut into quarters. Place tofu on a paper towel, sprinkle with salt, and let sit for 10 minutes. Wrap in paper towels to remove as much water as possible.

2. **Perilla leaves** Remove stems.
   Napa cabbage kimchi Lightly shake off the seasoning, squeeze firmly with your hands, and shred into 1.5 cm thick slices.

3. In a small bowl, mix the tofu seasoning ingredients. In another bowl, mix the kimchi seasoning ingredients.

4. Add cooking oil to a hot pan and cook tofu over medium heat for 2 minutes and 30 seconds on each side. Add the tofu seasoning, reduce the heat to medium-low and cook, flipping, for 2 to 3 minutes, then set aside.

5. Wash and reheat the pan and stir-fry the kimchi and kimchi seasoning ingredients over medium-low heat for 2 minutes. Turn off the heat and let cool slightly.

Seasoning the Cooked Rice

In a large bowl, mix the cooked rice and the rice seasoning ingredients, then let cool slightly.

Enjoy It Non-spicy

Wash the existing kimchi seasoning thoroughly under running water and squeeze the water out by hand. Omit the red pepper powder from the kimchi seasoning ingredients and follow the same steps the rest of the way.

Rolling the Kimbap

Spread the cooked rice (½ portion) ¾ of the way across the laver.

↓

Spread 2 perilla leaves and top with tofu (½ portion).

↓

Top with kimchi (½ portion).

↓

Wrap the ingredients with the perilla leaves and roll up.

↓

Make 1 more roll and cut into bite-sized pieces.

Make It Extra Special

Using Side Dishes from the Fridge as Kimbap Ingredients

Using side dishes as fillings for kimbap is a great way to add more flavor—
and it's less prep work!

1
Ready-made side dishes for kimbap

Side dishes such as dried radish strips, egg rolls, garlic pickles, seasoned vegetables, stewed nuts, stir-fried anchovies, and stir-fried dried squid strips can be used in kimbap just as they are.

2
Usable side dishes after removing water

Drain side dishes such as cucumber pickles, *jangjorim*, perilla leaf pickles, red pepper pickles, and seasoned bean sprouts in a sieve, then squeeze them tightly by hand to remove any leftover water before adding any of them to your kimbap.

3
Side dishes that need to be washed or re-cooked

Side dishes such as kimchi, *mukeunji*, and pollock roe can also be used as ingredients for kimbap. Lightly rinse the kimchi or *mukeunji* under running water to remove the seasoning, squeeze out the water, shred finely, and toss it with sugar and sesame oil. You can also add stir-fried kimchi according to your taste. Rinse the pollock roe, remove the tough outer tissue, and use the roe only (see page 85).

For very salty side dishes, reduce or omit the salt when seasoning the cooked rice and use only sesame seeds and sesame oil. You can roll the finished kimbap in *gomchwi* or cabbage to reduce the saltiness (see pages 101 and 109).

CHAPTER 4

Extra Spicy Kimbap

Challenge Your Taste Buds Using Korean Spices!

Spicy Yakgochujang Kimbap

The crunchiness of cucumber and the spiciness of *gochujang* are harmonized in this type of kimbap. Wrapping the ingredients in lettuce first and then rolling it all in laver helps to keep the kimbap firm. It also keeps the seasoning from getting on the rice, ensuring it doesn't look messy.

⏱ **30–40 minutes / 2 rolls (1 roll = 409 kcal)**

- 1½ bowls (300 g) warm cooked rice
- 2 laver sheets
- 100 g minced beef
- ¼ cucumber
- 2 Cheongyang chili peppers
- 4 lettuce leaves (or other leafy vegetables)
- ½ tsp sesame oil
- 1 Tbsp sesame seeds
- ½ Tbsp sugar
- 1½ Tbsp *gochujang*

Base Seasoning
- 1 Tbsp refined rice wine (or *soju*)
- a pinch of ground black pepper

Cooked Rice Seasoning
- 1 Tbsp sesame seeds
- 1 Tbsp sesame oil
- ⅓ tsp salt

Preparing the Ingredients

1. **Cucumber** Remove seeds and finely shred (see page 25).
   ▶ Add raw cucumber so that its crunchiness and moisture combine well with the spicy flavor of *yakgochujang*.

2. **Ground beef** Wrap it in a paper towel to drain the blood, then toss it with the base seasoning ingredients and let sit for 5 minutes.

3. **Lettuce** Wash under running water and shake off the water.
   Cheongyang chili pepper Finely mince.

4. Add sesame oil to a hot pan, add ground beef and stir-fry over medium-low heat for 2 minutes while breaking it up with a spatula, then add sesame seeds, sugar, and *gochujang*, and stir-fry for a further 3 minutes.

5. Turn off the heat and stir in the Cheongyang chili pepper.

Seasoning the Cooked Rice

In a large bowl, mix the cooked rice and the rice seasoning ingredients, then let cool slightly.

Enjoy It Non-spicy

Proceed to step ③, omitting the Cheongyang chili pepper, and add 1⅓ tsp sugar, 2 tsp brewed soy sauce, and stir-fry over medium heat for 1 minute. Then add 1 Tbsp sesame seeds and stir-fry 1 more minute. Roll tighter than usual, as the ingredients will be easier to spread without *gochujang*.

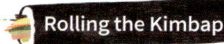

Rolling the Kimbap

Spread the cooked rice (½ portion) ¾ of the way across the laver.

↓

Spread 2 pieces of lettuce and top with the stir-fried beef (½ portion).

↓

Top with cucumber (½ portion).

↓

Wrap the lettuce around the ingredients first, then roll up.

↓

Make 1 more roll and cut into bite-sized pieces.

Chili Tuna Kimbap

A sweet and spicy twist on the popular tuna kimbap with a different sauce. Perilla leaves are used to get rid of the fishy flavor of tuna, and cucumber and yellow pickled radish are added for texture.

30–40 minutes / 2 rolls (1 roll = 403 kcal)

- 1½ bowls (300 g) warm cooked rice
- 2 laver sheets
- 1 canned tuna (small size, 100 g)
- ¼ cucumber (cut lengthwise)
- 4 strips braised burdock root (see page 25 for cooking)
- 2 strips yellow pickled radish
- 4 perilla leaves
- a pinch of salt

Tuna Seasoning

- 2 Cheongyang chili peppers, minced
- 1 Tbsp sweet chili sauce
- 1½ Tbsp mayonnaise
- 2 tsp hot sauce

Cooked Rice Seasoning

- 2 tsp sesame seeds
- ⅓ tsp salt
- 2 tsp sesame oil

Preparing the Ingredients

1. **Tuna** Drain in a sieve, pressing down with the back of a spoon to remove the oil, and mix with the tuna seasoning ingredients.
   Yellow pickled radish Drain in a sieve, rinse under running water, and remove any leftover water.
   Perilla leaves Remove stems.

2. **Braised burdock root** Wash under running water to reduce the saltiness, then remove any leftover water.

3. **Cucumber** Remove seeds, cut into long strips (see no. 1 on page 25 for preparing cucumber), toss with salt, and let sit for 5 minutes. Place in a sieve and rinse under cold water, then wrap in paper towels to remove any leftover water.

Seasoning the Cooked Rice

In a large bowl, mix the cooked rice and the rice seasoning ingredients, then let cool slightly.

Enjoy It Non-spicy

Omit the Cheongyang chili peppers and hot sauce from the tuna seasoning ingredients. You can also add 1 thick egg strip (see page 28) according to your taste.

Rolling the Kimbap

Spread the cooked rice (½ portion) ¾ of the way across the laver.

↓

Spread 2 perilla leaves and top with tuna (½ portion).

↓

Top with 1 strip cucumber and 2 strips burdock root.

↓

Top with 1 strip yellow pickled radish and roll up.

↓

Make 1 more roll and cut into bite-sized pieces.

Hot Squid Kimbap

Hot squid stir-fried in a spicy *gochujang* sauce with tangy garlic chives. The squid is stir-fried with sugar to infuse it with sweetness. It has barely any water, making it a perfect filling for kimbap.

35–45 minutes / 2 rolls (1 roll = 485 kcal)
- 1½ bowls (300 g) warm cooked rice
- 2 laver sheets
- 1 squid (240 g, after prep 180 g)
- 1 fistful garlic chives
  (or chives, water parsley, 50 g)
- 10 cm leek
- 1 Tbsp sugar
- 1½ Tbsp cooking oil

Garlic Chive Seasoning
- 1 tsp red pepper powder
- 1 tsp sesame oil

Squid Seasoning
- 3 Cheongyang chili peppers, minced
- 1 Tbsp red pepper powder
- 1 tsp minced garlic
- 2 tsp brewed soy sauce
- 2 tsp *gochujang*
- a pinch of ground black pepper

Cooked Rice Seasoning
- 2 tsp sesame seeds
- ½ tsp salt
- 2 tsp sesame oil

Preparing the Ingredients

1. **Squid** Prepare (see page 12). Cut the body in two, lengthwise, and into 0.5 cm thick slices, then cut the legs into 5 cm long slices.

2. **Leek** Chop into small pieces.
   Garlic chives Cut into 2 pieces and lightly toss in garlic chive seasoning.
   In a bowl, combine the squid seasoning ingredients.

3. Add cooking oil to a hot pan, stir-fry leek over medium heat for 1 minute, then add squid and sugar to stir-fry for 2 minutes. Add squid seasoning, reduce heat to medium-low, and stir-fry for 2 minutes.

Seasoning the Cooked Rice

In a large bowl, mix the cooked rice and the rice seasoning ingredients, then let cool slightly.

Rolling the Kimbap

Spread the cooked rice (½ portion) ¾ of the way across the laver.

↓

Top with squid (½ portion).

↓

Top with garlic chives (½ portion) and roll up.

↓

Make 1 more roll and cut into bite-sized pieces.

Add Cheese

You can also add sliced cheese (2 slices) to neutralize the spiciness.

Add Ssammu

You can also add some *ssammu* (8 slices) for a sweet and sour flavor.

Spicy Fish Cake Kimbap

Try stir-frying these chewy, flavorful fish cakes in spicy seasonings and adding them to kimbap for a delicious meal.

⏱ **40–50 minutes / 2 rolls (1 roll = 454 kcal)**
- 1½ bowls (300 g) warm cooked rice
- 2 laver sheets
- 2 rectangular sheets fish cake
- ½ cucumber
- 2 eggs
- 2 strips yellow pickled radish
- 4 perilla leaves
- a pinch of salt + ¼ tsp salt
- 1 tsp cooking oil

Fish Cake Seasoning
- 1 Cheongyang chili pepper (or green chili pepper)
- 2 tsp red pepper powder
- ½ tsp minced garlic
- 1 tsp brewed soy sauce
- 1 tsp *gochujang*
- 1 tsp oligofructose
- 2 tsp sesame oil

Cooked Rice Seasoning
- 2 tsp sesame seeds
- ⅓ tsp salt
- 2 tsp sesame oil

Preparing the Ingredients

1. **Eggs** In a bowl, whisk the eggs and a pinch of salt.
   Perilla leaves Remove stems.
   Yellow pickled radish Place in sieve and rinse under running water, then remove any leftover water.
   Cheongyang chili pepper Chop into small pieces.
   Fish cake Shred into 0.5 cm thick slices.

2. **Cucumber** Remove seeds and shred finely; toss with salt (¼ tsp) and let sit for 10 minutes. Drain in a sieve, rinse under cold water, and wrap in paper towels to remove any leftover water (see page 25).

3. In a bowl, combine the fish cake seasoning ingredients, then add fish cake and mix.

4. See page 29 to make shredded egg.

5. Wipe out the pan, add ③ and stir-fry over medium heat for 2 minutes.

Seasoning the Cooked Rice

In a large bowl, mix the cooked rice and the rice seasoning ingredients, then let cool slightly.

Enjoy It Non-spicy

You can substitute the fish cake seasoning with ½ tsp minced garlic + 2 tsp brewed soy sauce + 1 tsp oligofructose, and 40 g coarsely minced almonds, then roll together.

Rolling the Kimbap

Spread the cooked rice (½ portion) ¾ of the way across the laver.

↓

Spread 2 perilla leaves and top with shredded cucumber (½ portion).

↓

Top with shredded egg strips (½ portion) and shredded fish cake (½ portion).

↓

Top with 1 strip yellow pickled radish and roll up.

↓

Make 1 more roll and cut into bite-sized pieces.

Myeolchu Kimbap

Myeolchu means anchovy + chili pepper, and it's seasoned with *gochujang*, which goes well with anchovies, making it perfect for mini kimbap, which can be eaten in one bite, rather than regular-sized kimbap.

⏱ 25–35 minutes / 8 pieces (1 piece = 79 kcal)
- 1½ bowls (300 g) warm cooked rice
- 2 laver sheets
- 4 Cheongyang chili peppers (or green chili pepper)
- 30 g small anchovies
- 1 Tbsp cooking oil
- 1 Tbsp *gochujang*
- 1 tsp sugar

Preparing the Ingredients

1. **Laver** Cut into quarters.
   Cheongyang chili peppers Halve, remove seeds, and finely mince.

2. Add cooking oil to a hot pan and stir-fry the small anchovies over medium heat for 3 minutes, add the minced Cheongyang chili peppers, and stir-fry for 1 minute.

3. Turn off the heat and add the cooked rice, *gochujang*, and sugar, mixing evenly.

4. Return to high heat and stir-fry for 1 minute, then spread out and let cool slightly.

Rolling the Kimbap

Spread the seasoned cooked rice (⅛ portion) ¾ of the way across the laver.

↓

Roll up.
Make 4 more rolls.

Enjoy It Non-spicy

Omit the Cheongyang chili peppers and *gochujang*. In step ③, stir-fry with 1 tsp brewed soy sauce and 1 tsp oligofructose, then turn off the heat and add 1 tsp sesame oil.

Spicy Nuts Kimbap

Sweet stir-fried small anchovies & nuts and green pepper pickles give this kimbap a sweet & spicy yet refreshing flavor. The soft, shredded egg strips and spinach go well with the firm texture of the stir-fried anchovies & nuts.

⏱ 30–40 minutes / 2 rolls (1 roll = 539 kcal)

- 1½ bowls (300 g) warm cooked rice
- 2 laver sheets
- 1½ fistfuls spinach (75 g)
- 4 Tbsp minced nuts
  (or walnuts/almonds, 40 g)
- 2 Tbsp small anchovies (10 g)
- 2 eggs
- 16 green pepper pickles
  (or jalapenos/chili pepper pickles, 30 g)
- 2 strips yellow pickled radish
- a pinch of salt
- 2 tsp sesame oil
- 1½ tsp oligofructose
- 2 tsp cooking oil

Cooked Rice Seasoning

- 4 strips burdock root
  (see page 25 for cooking, optional)
- 2 tsp sesame seeds
- ⅓ tsp salt
- 2 tsp sesame oil

Preparing the Ingredients

1. **Spinach** Blanch in boiling water (3 cups water + 1 tsp salt) for 30 seconds, then rinse in cold water and squeeze out water. In a bowl, toss the spinach, salt (a little), and sesame oil.

2. **Green pepper pickles** Drain in a sieve, remove stems and squeeze out water by hand.
   Yellow pickled radish Drain in a sieve, rinse under running water, then remove any leftover water.

3. **Eggs** In a bowl, whisk the eggs and a pinch of salt.
   See page 29 to make shredded egg.

4. Add 1 tsp cooking oil to a hot pan, add anchovies and stir-fry over medium-low heat for 2 minutes, add nuts and stir-fry for 1 minute, then turn off the heat. Add the oligofructose and mix lightly.
   ▶ Stir-fry small anchovies first to get rid of the fishy flavor.

Seasoning the Cooked Rice

Braised burdock root Finely mince.
In a large bowl, mix the cooked rice and the rice seasoning ingredients.

Using Gochujang Sauce

Add 1 tsp chili oil to a hot pan, then add ½ tsp minced garlic, anchovies, and stir-fry over medium-low heat for 2 minutes. Add nuts and stir-fry for 1 minute, turn off the heat, then mix in 1 tsp *gochujang* and 1 tsp oligofructose.

Rolling the Kimbap

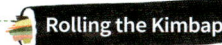

Spread the cooked rice (½ portion) ¾ of the way across the laver.

↓

Add stir-fried anchovies & nuts (½ portion) and spinach (½ portion).

↓

Top with shredded egg strips (½ portion) and green pepper pickles (½ portion).

↓

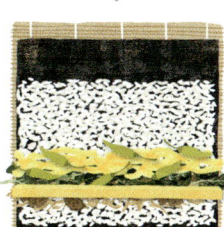

Add 1 strip yellow pickled radish and roll up.

↓

Make 1 more roll and cut into bite-sized pieces.

Ttaengcho Kimbap

Ttaengcho kimbap is a famous delicacy from the Jinju region. It's made by tossing soft and fluffy cooked rice with soy sauce and spicy minced Cheongyang chili peppers, making it the perfect dish for hot summer days. It's bite-sized, which makes it even more appealing for eating while on the go.

⏱ **20–30 minutes / 3 rolls (1 roll = 225 kcal)**

- 1½ bowls (300 g) cooked rice
- 3 laver sheets
- 2 Cheongyang chili peppers
- ⅕ carrot
- 1 Tbsp sesame seeds
- 2 Tbsp sesame oil

Ttaengcho Soy Sauce
- 1 Cheongyang chili pepper
- 1 Tbsp water
- 1 Tbsp brewed soy sauce
- ½ tsp sugar
- ⅓ tsp minced garlic

Preparing the Ingredients

1. **Cheongyang chili pepper (for soy sauce)**
   Cut into quarters.
   In a small saucepan, combine the soy sauce ingredients and simmer over low heat for 4 minutes.

2. **Laver sheet** Remove ⅓ of a standard-sized laver sheet.
   Carrot Finely mince.
   Cheongyang chili pepper (for cooked rice)
   Halve two chili peppers, remove the seeds, and finely mince.

Seasoning the Cooked Rice

In a large bowl, mix the cooked rice, soy sauce, minced Cheongyang chili peppers, carrot, sesame seeds, and sesame oil, then let cool slightly.

Rolling the Kimbap

Spread the cooked rice (⅓ portion) ¾ of the way across the laver.

↓

Roll up.
Make 2 more rolls and cut each into thirds.

Enjoy It Non-spicy

You can substitute the Cheongyang chili peppers in the ingredients with an equal amount of green chili peppers. If choosing to do this, omit the Cheongyang chili peppers in the soy sauce.

Make It Extra Special

Soups to Pair with Spicy Kimbap

Here's a selection of nice soups to soothe your stomach when eating spicy kimbap.

Deeply flavored Mushroom & Garlic Chive Soup

⏱ 35–45 minutes / 1 serving = 53 kcal
- 6 shiitake mushrooms
- 1 fistful garlic chives (50 g)
- ¼ onion (50 g)
- ½ tsp salt
  (add or subtract as desired)
- a pinch of ground black pepper
- ½ tsp sesame oil

Stock
- 5 sheets 3×3 cm kelp
- 4 pieces 10 cm leek (green part)
- 3 cloves garlic
- 5 cups water (1.25 ℓ)

Seasoning
- 2 Tbsp minced leek
- 1 Tbsp minced garlic
- 1½ Tbsp soy sauce for soup

❶ Combine the shiitake mushrooms and stock ingredients in a saucepan. Bring to a boil over high heat, reduce to medium-low heat, and simmer for 5 minutes. Scoop out the kelp and simmer for another 10 minutes, and then scoop out the other solid ingredients. Set aside the shiitake mushrooms.

❷ Cut the garlic chives into 4 cm pieces and the onion into 0.5 cm thick slices.

❸ Let the shiitake mushrooms cool slightly, then remove the stems and slice into 1 cm thick slices.

❹ In a large bowl, mix the seasoning ingredients, add the shiitake mushrooms and onion, then toss.

❺ Add ④ to the saucepan from ① and bring to a boil over high heat, then reduce heat to medium and simmer for 10 minutes.

❻ Add the garlic chives, salt, and ground black pepper, and simmer over medium heat for 3 minutes. Then turn off the heat, add sesame oil, and mix.

Onion and Egg Soup for a quick and easy meal

⏱ **20–30 minutes / 1 serving = 120 kcal**
- 1 onion (200 g)
- 2 eggs
- 10 cm leek (green part)
- 1 tsp minced garlic
- 2 tsp salted shrimp
- ½ tsp salt
  (add or subtract as desired)

Stock
- 20 anchovies for stock (20 g)
- 2 sheets 5×5 cm kelp
- 3 pieces 10 cm leek (green part)
- 4 cups water (1 ℓ)

❶ Combine stock ingredients in a saucepan. Bring to a boil over high heat, reduce to medium-low heat, and simmer for 5 minutes. Scoop out the kelp and simmer for 10 minutes, then scoop out the anchovies and leek.
   ▶ This recipe makes 3 cups (750~800 ml) of stock. Add more water if needed.

❷ Chop the onion into 2×2 cm pieces and slice the leek into small pieces.

❸ Beat the egg in a bowl.

❹ Add the onion, minced garlic, and salted shrimp to the saucepan in ①, and then boil over medium heat for 2 minutes.

❺ Pour in the egg wash clockwise, and boil over medium heat for 30 seconds.
   ▶ Be careful not to stir right after pouring in the egg wash or the soup will turn out messy.

❻ Add the leek and salt, then simmer over medium heat, allowing it to boil for 30 seconds and stirring all the while.

Index

A
Addictive Kimbap • 88
Asparagus Kimbap • 56
Avocado & Crab Meat Kimbap • 72

B
Bassak Bulgogi & Water Parsley Kimbap • 66
Buckwheat Kimbap • 90
Burger Kimbap • 96

C
Chicken Breast & Coleslaw Kimbap • 54
Chili Tuna Kimbap • 122
Chungmu Kimbap • 114
Cucumber Cream Cheese Nude Kimbap • 82

D
Dried Radish Strips Kimbap • 108
Dried Squid Strip Kimbap • 112

E
Eel Kimbap • 78
Egg Roll Kimbap • 40

F
Family Kimbap • 52
Flower Kimbap • 58

G, H
Garlic Chives & Bacon Kimbap • 98
Hot Squid Kimbap • 124

J, K
Jangjorim Kimbap • 102
Jeyuk Ssam Kimbap • 100
Kabocha Squash & Tteokgalbi Kimbap • 60

M
Mini Kimbap • 44
Mukeunji Kimbap • 110
Myeolchu Kimbap • 128

N
Namul Kimbap • 86
Nude Kimbap • 38

O, P
Omelet Rice Kimbap • 70
Pollock Roe Kimbap • 84
Pork Cutlet Kimbap • 68
Premium King Kimbap • 36

R, S
Regular Kimbap • 32
Salmon Kimbap • 80
Seasoned Fried Chicken Kimbap • 94
Seasoned Yellow Pickled Radish Kimbap • 104
Smiley Kimbap • 62
Smoked Duck Nude Kimbap • 64
Spam Egg Roll • 106
Spicy Fish Cake Kimbap • 126
Spicy Nuts Kimbap • 130
Spicy Yakgochujang Kimbap • 120
Sprout Salad & Tuna Kimbap • 76
Square Kimbap • 44

T, W
Teriyaki Shrimp Kimbap • 74
Tofu Kimchi Kimbap • 116
Ttaengcho Kimbap • 132
Water Drop Kimbap • 42